Please renew/return this item by the last date shown.

So that your telephone call is charged at local rate,
please call the numbers as set out below:

	From Area codes 01923 or 0208:	From the rest of Herts:
Renewals:	01923 471373	01438 737373
Enquiries:	01923 471333	01438 737333
Minicom:	01923 471599	01438 737599

L32b

D1433286

A HISTORY OF
CROSVILLE
MOTOR SERVICES

R. C. ANDERSON

David & Charles
Newton Abbot   London   North Pomfret (Vt)

British Library Cataloguing in Publication Data

Anderson, R. C.
  A history of Crosville Motor Services.
  1. Crosville Motor Services – History
  I. Title
  388.3'22'09421   HE5664.Z7.C/

  ISBN 0–7153–8088–5

Typeset by
Northern Phototypesetting Co., Bolton
and printed in Great Britain by
Biddles Limited, Guildford
for David & Charles (Publishers) Limited
Brunel House, Newton Abbot, Devon

Published in the United States of America
by David & Charles Inc.
North Pomfret, Vermont 05053, USA

Contents

Introduction and Acknowledgements

Crosville is a bus company of remarkable contrasts, serving on the one hand in the north east of its territory as a suburban network, feeding into the Merseyside conurbation from areas in Cheshire beyond the Merseyside Passenger Transport Executive boundary, and on the other as a lifeline to remote villages in mountainous North Wales. Between, it serves industrial North East Wales around Wrexham and Shotton, and the seaside resorts along the North Wales coast and down the west coast as far south as Aberystwyth. Today, as part of the nationalised National Bus Company and one of the major bus concerns in the country, few outside the bus industry and certainly not many of Crosville's passengers would realise that it started as a small family business. It is the development of that family firm from its beginnings nearly 80 years ago into a major bus undertaking that forms the story in this book, covering the expansion of services, the buses themselves, and the personalities that ran the firm. Of course, within the confines of a general history space does not allow every single service change to be chronicled, nor, indeed, the history of every bus. The text, though, discusses the trends, the major route developments, the vehicle types and the history of the company in all its aspects.

I hope that those members of the Crosville staff who read this book will take time to consider how the imagination of one family, starting from nothing, led to the creation of this business, and perhaps it will give a greater insight into a number of matters with which they may not be familiar. It was my own good fortune to be engaged as a Crosville trainee, and having left the company at the end of my training to take up an appointment with another bus company, to return some eleven years later to be divisional manager at Crewe. Obviously some of the information contained in this history is from my own experience as an employee of Crosville but I would stress that the opinions in this book (unless stated otherwise) are mine and must not in any way be construed as representing the views, official or unofficial, of the National Bus Company or Crosville Motor Services Ltd.

Many independent operators still provide bus services within the Crosville operating area and their omission from this book in no way implies any lack of respect for the important contribution they make to the overall public transport scene.

I must acknowledge the value of the two histories of Crosville written by the late W. J. Crosland-Taylor, and then to record my thanks to David Meredith, general manager of Crosville Motor Services Ltd, for the help and encouragement that he has given me during the time I have been preparing this history. David Deacon, now retired, has been particularly helpful in advising me in regard to Crosville in the twenties and thirties and it was he who supplied much of the interesting details of the events surrounding the acquisition of the Western Transport Co. John Parker, a former colleague of mine who is still with Crosville, has gone to a great deal of trouble to answer my queries and he has supplied much useful information, for which I am extremely grateful. My thanks also to David Kirby who made available to me data from his private collection, to Bill Cunliffe who advised me in regard to vehicles, past and present, and to Bruce Smetham who assisted in sorting out the recent history of the Crosville fleet. I have also been helped by a number of other persons and organisations and although I have not mentioned them all by name their help has nonetheless been invaluable. Finally, my grateful appreciation of all the efforts made by Margaret Von Kaenel who struggled with my writing to make an excellent job of typing the manuscript.

Haytor, Devon   R. C. Anderson

1

Pioneering 1910 – 1929

George Crosland Taylor

George Crosland Taylor was born on Sunday 31 January 1857 the son of Henry Dyson Taylor, proprietor of the Worsted Coating Mill just outside of Huddersfield. His second Christian name 'Crosland' was his mother's maiden name – Sarah Crosland. By some peculiar chance he was always known as 'Crosland' and at the age of sixteen he started work at his father's mill. Always fascinated by machinery and chemistry, his particular interest was the development of electricity, and after a visit to the Paris Exhibition in 1881 he was able to establish in February 1882, at Weston in Cheshire, a firm known as G. C. Taylor & Co, to manufacture electrical machinery. In 1886 the business was transferred to Helsby, where it has remained ever since, and became known as the Telegraph Manufacturing Co. Since that time it has amalgamated with several other companies and often changed its name until today when it is known as BICC General Cables Ltd. In 1899 Taylor became interested in the newest development, the internal combustion engine, and was soon the owner of a 10hp Wolseley with horizontal twin-cylinder engine, chain-driven, and fitted with a four-seater body. Visits were made to the Paris Motor Show in 1903, 1904 and 1905 when he met a Frenchman called George Ville, from whom he purchased two sample cars in 1906 with a view to assembling and selling cars of French design. So it was in 1906 that a company was formed, the Crosville Motor Company Ltd, with premises at Crane Wharf, Chester, with George

7

Crosland Taylor as Chairman, although cars, and later buses, were of secondary interest to him, his prime concern being the electric cable-making firm. One of his three sons, Edward Crosland-Taylor, was employed in the business and became general manager on 23 June 1909 at a salary of £1-15-0d (£1.75) per week, having been employed from the beginning at £1 10s 0d (£1.50) per week. Losses were heavy, and the two directors were soon making loans in order to enable the business to be carried on. In September 1910 the other director, Mr C. B. Catt (he was the son of the other founder director, Mr C. W. Catt) resigned from the board and the situation was such that Crosland should have put the company into liquidation. Edward was appointed a director in place of Mr Catt and the business carried on, but in addition to the motor cars a bus service was commenced in January 1911 between Chester and Ellesmere Port. In its choice of route Crosville was fortunate insofar as it paid its way from the outset. Ellesmere Port was the port for Ellesmere, a small market town in Shropshire from which a branch of the Shropshire Union Canal linked the town with the Manchester Ship Canal by the side of the river Mersey. Ellesmere Port developed and when it was chosen as the site for an oil refinery then its future was assured. The townspeople wished to travel to Chester, Birkenhead and Liverpool, but to get to Chester by rail they had to change at Hooton and travel twelve miles, whereas by bus it was only eight. At about the same time Edward Crosland-Taylor emigrated to America and his place on the board was taken, at the request of his father, by his brother Claude Crosland-Taylor who had been working at the cable works.

First bus services

The introduction of the first bus services in 1911 between Chester and Ellesmere Port, Chester and Kelsall, and in 1913 from Nantwich to Crewe and Sandbach, followed in the same year by services from Ellesmere Port and Chester to New Ferry changed the financial position from loss-making to a profit in

April 1914 of £1,302. Then came World War I with an immediate requirement for buses to serve the new munitions factory established at Mold, and although some additional services in the Nantwich and Crewe area (including Crewe town services) were started in 1915 it was not generally possible to develop the business at this time. However, the company came out of the war in a profitable situation, with traffic receipts increasing from £6,041 in 1914 to £27,522 in 1918.

Road haulage

During 1912 the company commenced in road haulage and had several Daimler lorries to which were added four Foden steam wagons and trailers to overcome the petrol shortage. The company also entered the contract farming business with Crosville tractors being used to tow the ploughs, but in 1919 it was decided to discontinue these aspects of the business in favour of expanded bus operation. Accordingly the equipment was entered in a Manchester auction and the Fodens sold for an average of £1,750 each.

Nantwich depot

Nantwich depot had been opened in 1915 and when in 1919 W. J. Crosland-Taylor was demobilised from the Royal Marines he too joined the company, becoming a director in October 1919 with an arrangement that Claude Crosland-Taylor would look after the head office and W. J. Crosland-Taylor would control the day-to-day operations. As a result W. J. Crosland-Taylor went to Nantwich and subsequently to Mold, Warrington and West Kirby as developments took place in these areas. Some local authorities licensed vehicles, but not services, so once these were obtained any route could be opened up. Other authorities had never adopted the bye-laws relating to hackney carriages, and emergent bus companies ran anywhere in the area without the need to obtain any sort of licence or permission. After travelling over a route by car, taking the mileage and deciding on the timetable and fare stages, handbills were printed announcing details of the service, and distributed to every house within one half mile of the route. Generally one bus and crew was used to establish a service to which it was allocated.

Competition

The Chester to Ellesmere Port service had been extended to New Ferry on a two-hourly frequency when in September 1919 Mr J. M. Hudson commenced a competing service between Chester and Ellesmere Port, to which he added another service between the same places but via Stoke and Upton with additional 'shorts' between Upton and Chester on Saturdays. Ellesmere Port UDC granted a licence but Chester Corporation refused Mr Hudson's application. He got over this by picking-up and setting-down his passengers in Chester on private ground at the *Coach and Horses* Hotel in the Market Square. Subsequently he was given a licence by Chester Corporation and then the real competition began, with Crosville painting a bus blue to represent those operated by Mr Hudson and cutting fares. This was cut-throat competition, with drivers cutting-in and attempting to force each other off the road. This lasted throughout 1921 and in the end Ellesmere Port council stepped in and asked both operators to come to some agreement, failing which the council would take steps to stop both of them running. As a result Mr Hudson's business went into liquidation on 27 January 1922 and in the following month Mr Hudson joined Crosville as the private hire department manager.

Extended tours

'Joe' Hudson was to be responsible for organising Crosville's venture into the field of extended tours, in which activity they were early on the scene. The first tours were undertaken in 1928 with departures being offered to Devon, Scotland, the Lake District and the Midlands; this last tour was discontinued after operations in 1929, but in 1931 the South Coast was added to the programme. There were no further changes until 1935 when departures to the East Coast were added, and in 1936–38 tours to the Midlands were tried again but abandoned after operations in 1938. Scotland was the most popular destination, followed by Devon and the South Coast. The East Coast came next, then the English Lakes and the least popular was the Midlands. In those days when inflation was not a feature of everyday life the average cost of a week's tour, manned by two drivers, was £10. The success of the British tours led Crosville to consider continental tours and arrangements were made with the Deutche Reichsbahn (German State Railways) for hotel reservations in Germany, with provision for basing a Crosville coach in Cologne to work different tours from there each week throughout the season. Passengers would be transferred from Britain to Cologne by air or rail and boat dependent on the preference of the individual. The intention was to commence in 1938 but the worsening political situation in Germany meant that the continental tours did not materialise and, of course, the British tours ceased after 1939. With the end of the war in 1945 Crosville decided not to resume the extended tours and the licences were taken up by Salopia of Whitchurch.

Death of George Crosland Taylor

George Crosland Taylor had never been very strong owing to the weakness of one lung and he died on 12 January 1923. Claude Crosland-Taylor was appointed in his place as chairman of what was an expanding family concern. Another change was the appointment of outside shareholders to the board, particularly as it was evident that the programme of expansion was going to require new capital each year for some time in the future.

Post World War I expansion

Meanwhile new bus services had been commenced in a variety of areas. Chester was linked with Warrington in 1919 and in the following year the Chester–Crewe–Newcastle service had

11

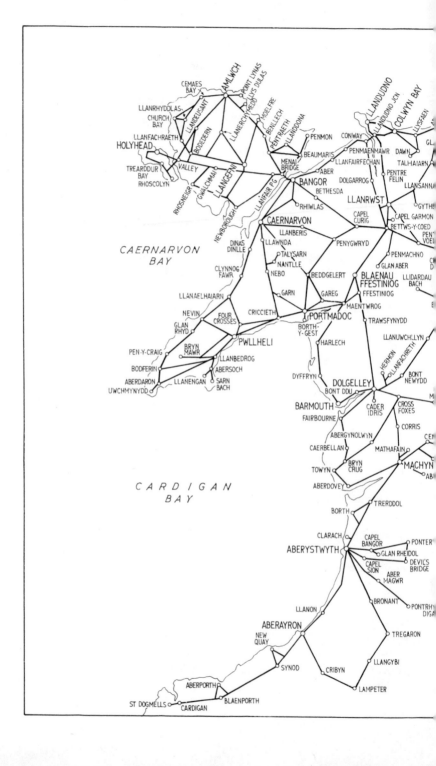

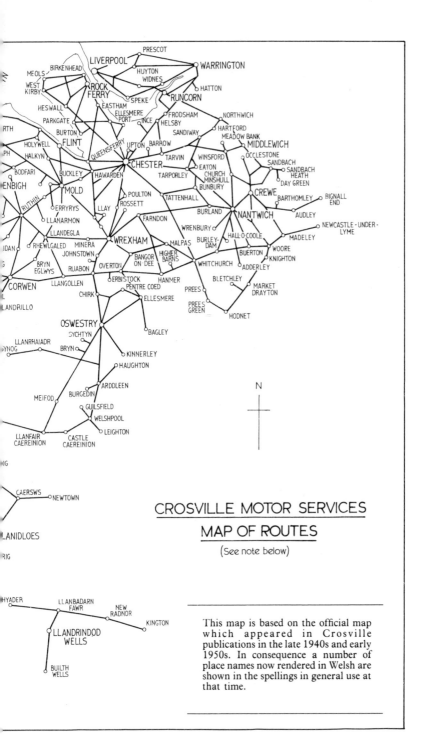

CROSVILLE MOTOR SERVICES

MAP OF ROUTES

(See note below)

This map is based on the official map which appeared in Crosville publications in the late 1940s and early 1950s. In consequence a number of place names now rendered in Welsh are shown in the spellings in general use at that time.

commenced. Services in Flint and Mold had also been started in 1919 and in the West Kirby area in 1920 including one to Birkenhead (Bidston Hill) which was extended to Park Station in 1924. It was clear then that the bus services in the Wirral, Cheshire and South West Lancashire would be the foundation of the company and to them would be added the services into north and central Wales in addition to those already commenced and being extended in the Mold and Flint areas. It is interesting to note that the first such services were started in 1922 between Llanrwst and Rhyl and Llanrwst and Ruthin; I suspect that these may have been operated by a vehicle from Mold which had begun operating through to Ruthin in 1919 by way of extension to Llanrwst and then to Rhyl. The next stages of development came in the Aberystwyth and Llandrindod Wells areas, where services commenced in 1924 as did those in Blaenau Ffestiniog, the first route being from Porthmadog. This route operated in competition with the Festiniog Railway which from 1 July 1934 leased the dying Welsh Highland Railway. This arrangement, together with the competing Crosville buses, almost killed the Festiniog system, the final blow being the outbreak of World War II on 3 September 1939 with the result that rail traffic ceased entirely on 2 August 1946. Happily, through the efforts of railway preservation groups and energetic management the Festiniog Railway has re-opened and is now one of the major tourist attractions of North Wales.

Mid Cheshire and Crewe

The year 1923 brought problems in Cheshire where Crosville had been unsuccessful in 1912 in its application for licences in Northwich, which had resulted in the formation of a company named the Mid Cheshire Motor Bus Company Ltd. On 4 October 1923 Claude and W. J. Crosland-Taylor met the directors of the Mid Cheshire at Chester to discuss a possible take-over by Crosville, but there was a big difference in the asking price and what Crosville thought the business was worth, with the result that in the following year Mid-Cheshire sold out to the North Western Road Car Company Ltd. Competition erupted on the Crewe to Nantwich route when a man named Jim Gibson obtained licences and started running a Ford 14-seater just in front of the Crosville buses and taking the passengers. Although there was no price war Crosville put on a faster bus with the result that Gibson bought even faster buses and there were several 'incidents' including a deliberate collision between two buses in Prince Albert Street, Crewe, one Saturday night. To increase the tempo of competition Crosville modified a Leyland (No. 72) to go even faster and in the end, in April 1925, Crosville bought Gibson's business. There had also been competition at Crewe during World War I with a former engine driver named Gregory who ran a Clarkson steam bus, but he had been bought-out in 1915. Another business in the Crewe area, that of D. Taylor and Harry Peach of Haslington, was purchased in 1927.

All was quiet until 1929 when Sam Jackson and his sons commenced a service between Nantwich and Crewe, and this time it was war to the death with all the usual incidents to which was added 'fare cutting' to such an extent that the return fare between Nantwich and Crewe was down to 4d (1½p). Both Crosville and Jackson lost money, but the Road Traffic Act of 1930 resulted in both timetables and fares being placed on a proper footing, and in 1934 S. Jackson and Sons sold out to Crosville. Crosville's establishment in the Crewe area might have been very different if the BET had not withdrawn its 1897 application for a tramway in the town entirely on public roads just as it was about to be granted. It had caused considerable controversy as to whether a tramway type line could be authorised under the 1896 Light Railway Act: this one very nearly became the first. Subsequently Crewe Corporation twice applied unsuccessfully for tramway powers and the BET also had another try, but to no avail. Routes proposed were from Haslington via the railway station to Nantwich, with branches linking this route to the Square, with extensions via the Railway Works to Merrils Bridge and to the *Cross Keys* Hotel.

Birkenhead Corporation

Birkenhead Park Station had been reached by Crosville in 1924. This was a very important step because it connected with Liverpool via the Mersey Electric Railway. It had not, however, been achieved without a struggle that had started in 1923 when Crosville had fought Birkenhead Corporation in Parliament over a Bill which would have given the corporation powers to run anywhere outside the borough with the Minister of Transport's consent. As Crosville was already operating just outside the borough, the company was greatly relieved when Birkenhead's Bill was thrown out. In 1926 the borough had another try, but this time seeking powers to run anywhere within a five-mile radius. Crosville objected and out of it came an agreement dated 15 March 1926 between the company and the corporation which dealt specifically with services in the Moreton, Upton, Woodchurch and Prenton areas. A more far-reaching agreement between the two parties dated 6 June 1930 resulted in the Crosville services operating to New Ferry being extended to Woodside in the summer of that year, and those operating to Singleton Avenue in the autumn of that year. For its part, Birkenhead Corporation commenced operating from 1 October 1930 the Crosville service from Heswall via Irby to Singleton Avenue which was extended, on the same date, through to Woodside. Crosville services from West Kirby continued to terminate at Park Station, with the exception of the service from West Kirby via Irby Mill Hill which operated to Woodside. It must be recorded that Birkenhead obtained the best of the deal because Crosville was not permitted to take-up and set-down the same passengers within the agreed area, which in the Chester direction extended as far as Eastham. Another agreement in 1925, this time with Wallasey Corporation, resulted in Crosville buses running through to Liscard Village.

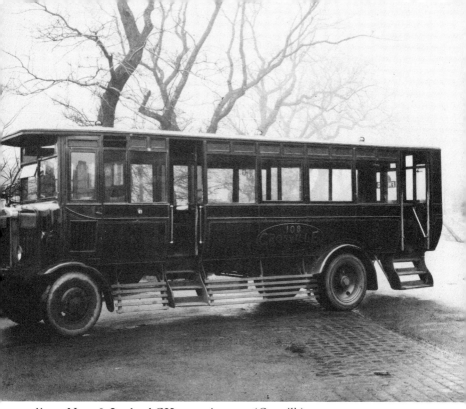

Above: No 108, Leyland GH7, new in 1923. (*Crosville*)

Below: Tilling B10A2 ex Western Transport in 1933 and numbered 867 (later R35) in the Crosville fleet. (*Crosville*)

Above: Leyland PLSC3 Lion, new to Crosville in 1928. (*C. Shears*)

Below: Leyland Titan TD1 in Crosville/LMS livery, new in 1930. (*Crosville*)

Merseyside

The haphazard situation which prevailed, with no uniform system of licencing, is well illustrated by the case of Warrington Corporation who imposed a toll of 1½d (1p) per passenger conveyed either in full or in part over any of its routes, an arrangement which lasted until 1931 when the Traffic Commissioners overruled it and substituted an ordinary limitation on picking-up and setting-down in the corporation's area. The year 1927 saw an agreement with Widnes Corporation which allowed Crosville to pick-up and set-down as the company liked, paying the corporation an agreed fee for each passenger conveyed. Both Warrington and Widnes were important to Crosville because it was in this direction that the company approached the highly-populated area of Liverpool. The first service from Warrington was to Prescott (1921) followed by another via Widnes (1921), while others in the area commenced in 1922 and 1923. Some services terminated at Garston where passengers had to continue their journey by Liverpool Corporation tram, and others at Edge Lane depot where a similar transfer of passengers took place. Eventually Crosville obtained a stand at the old Customs House by giving to the corporation tram services fare protection by way of a 6d (2½p) single or return minimum protective fare into Liverpool with absolute protection in the city. In due course the service from Warrington via Prescott was extended to Mount Pleasant, whereas that via Widnes terminated at Canning Place.

The Road Traffic Act 1930 became law in February 1931 but before that date, on 3 July 1930, there had been a meeting with the corporation attended by representatives of Ribble and the LMSR and LNER, but not Crosville, at which it was generally agreed that Liverpool Corporation should operate all the bus services in the city and share other services to places up to three miles outside the city area. Beyond these places were to be served by the provincial bus companies concerned. This agreement was implemented in general terms on 2 July 1931 and Crosville had a terminus at Liverpool Pier Head together with permission to pick up all local passengers in the city at a minimum fare of 4d ($1\frac{1}{2}$p) of which 30% was payable to Liverpool Corporation . The agreement was to last for five years and as Liverpool Corporation was having difficulties with its buses, Crosville ran the Brodie Avenue service on its behalf, paying the corporation 20% of the fares collected. The original agreement was renewed, with minor modifications, in 1936.

Chester Corporation

Crosville had problems, however, in Chester, whose corporation promoted a Bill in 1929 to replace its trams with buses, for in it they sought powers to operate within a ten-mile radius of Chester. This would have involved Ellesmere Port and as a result of Crosville's objection the radius was reduced to $3\frac{1}{2}$ miles, which enabled the corporation to extend its services to places never served by trams. The corporation's first buses came on the road in February 1930 and on 1 July 1932 both Crosville and Chester Corporation signed an agreement in regard to areas and routes to be served by the two undertakings.

Colwills and Croscols

In addition to the development of Crosville, the Crosland-Taylor family was involved during the twenties in two Devon bus undertakings, namely Colwills (Ilfracombe) Ltd from February 1920 and Croscols of Tiverton (a subsidiary of both Crosville and Colwills). However, the family gave up its interest in these companies in 1924. (Further details are included in *A History of Western National* by the author and G. G. A. Frankis).

Expansion in Wales

By 1929 Crosville was operating on the north coast of Wales, through Rhyl down to Bangor, with the area to Holywell already served from the Chester and Mold directions. A small business was purchased in Caernarfon and the routes were developed in connection with others already established to try to close the west side of the area, so that the operators could not expand onto new routes out of the area in which they were involved. The same technique had been applied in Central Wales, down the Cambrian coast as far as Cardigan.

However, the area was large in size but small in population, and although the wage rate in the Welsh areas was lower than in the more remunerative areas, until 1942 the Welsh services barely paid their way, even in those far-off days. To quote from Mr W. J. Crosland-Taylor's book *State Owned Without Tears* in regard to this situation:

> By 1929 we had this large area in square miles, but small in population, for which we had paid nothing and which barely paid its way. What was the best thing to do? It might have been better if it had been sold and the profits used to buy something better but we decided to adopt a policy of keeping it and buying certain other businessess where the goodwill paid for would be at least partially balanced by the economies that could be made by amalgamation.

There was to be further expansion in Wales, but this came in the thirties and is dealt with in chapter 2.

Express services

Crosville's express services on the North Wales coast originated from what would now be described as 'limited stop services' or 'long-distance stage carriage services', the first of these being commenced in 1923 between New Ferry, Queensferry and Mold. In 1925 this service was extended to Loggerheads where Crosville established a popular picnic and leisure site (see chapter 10). Other services were started, and on 8 July 1926 a daily summer service was introduced between Liverpool and Loggerheads via Chester and Mold utilising the Widnes – Runcorn transporter bridge to cross the Mersey River. A Birkenhead (Woodside) – Holywell express service was commenced in 1930, but this and the Woodside – Loggerheads and the Woodside (previously Birkenhead, Park Station) –

Denbigh services eventually became stage carriage services. Other services had been commenced as early as 1926 from the Wirral to Prestatyn and Rhyl, subsequently extended to Llandudno and in 1927 from Chester to Blackpool. UNU (see chapter 2) had commenced a Caernarfon – Birkenhead (Woodside) service in 1929 and with the acquisition of this business Crosville commenced operating this service with the benefit that the bulk of the traffic would originate in Merseyside rather than in North Wales, Birkenhead Watch Committee, having refused UNU a licence to take up originating passengers in Birkenhead, a facility now granted to Crosville. A further development of considerable significance was the operation of this service from 1930 on an 'all-the-year-round' basis. From December 1930 it was extended to commence at Liverpool (Edge Lane Crosville garage), coaches picking up in Liverpool and crossing the Mersey by ferry to Birkenhead (Woodside). At the same time two routes were inaugurated. Service 'A' operated via Holywell, St Asaph, Colwyn Bay, Conwy and Bangor. An alternative was the route via the coastal towns, and service 'B' was routed inland via Corwen and Betwys-y-coed to Bangor. Crosville still had competition on the North Wales routes, including Macdonalds (trading as Maxways) which had a co-ordination agreement with Crosville and the Wirral Motor Transport Co. The Crosville/Maxways agreement was terminated in 1933. On 10 February 1934 Crosville acquired the Wirral Motor Transport Co and on 30 November 1934 the Maxways business was purchased, Harry Macdonald joining the staff of Crosville.

A limited service to London, again from Birkenhead, was started in August 1928 and operated for a few weekends, to be followed by a regular service from 28 March 1929. On the same day James Pearson & Sons introduced a service from Liverpool to London, and there was considerable competition between the two operators. Crosville's original service (via Crewe and Stratford-on-Avon) was followed from 16 May 1929 by a second service, this time originating in Liverpool and routed via Warrington and St Albans. A number of other operators were involved in Liverpool – London services. There were considerable changes in combination of places served, while a very important event was the opening by London Coastal Coaches Ltd of Victoria Coach Station in Buckingham Palace Road, London. In May 1935 Crosville obtained the former Pearson business and with all the other competition 'off the road' had the route to itself from 1 June 1935. All services served Stratford, the principle one being that via Whitchurch, the other via Crewe and Newcastle-under-Lyme being operated during the summer only. There was also a Southport – London night service, but when express services were resumed after World War II this service was truncated at Liverpool.

Railway Bus services

It is not perhaps generally appreciated that many of the bus services introduced in the twenties by Crosville and smaller operators (many of whose services passed to Crosville with the purchase of their businesses) were in fact pioneered by the railway companies before World War I. This conflict caused their withdrawal, but had the railway companies resumed bus operations on the routes previously operated the future of Crosville, and indeed road passenger transport in Britain, would have been very different. The first bus service, for instance, between Birkenhead (Park Station) and Heswall was operated on Sundays only from January 1905 by the Mersey Railway, together with two other routes in Birkenhead. As a result of legal proceedings instituted by Birkenhead Corporation, the Mersey Railway (which was the only railway company to be involved in litigation in regard to early railway-operated bus services) ceased bus operation in 1906 but made a further attempt with a Rock Ferry station – Port Sunlight service in 1907, and then abandoned all efforts to work buses.

However, the London & North Western Railway commenced bus operations on 10 July 1905 with a service from Mold to Connah's Quay in Flint. The next bus service to be introduced in Wales was introduced on 11 October 1905 between Holywell railway station (later Holywell Junction) and Holywell (King's Head). Further bus services were introduced in this area, including one started on 27 July 1908, between Mold and Loggerheads tea-gardens, and on 1 March 1910 a service between Llandudno Junction, Colwyn Bay and Old Colwyn. Further bus services were introduced in 1911, between Conwy and Llanrwst via Trefriw, with subsequent developments in the Llanrwst/Betws-y-Coed area which, incidentally, had been served during the summer since 1908 with a bus service from Corwen, operated by the Great Western Railway. Various modifications were made to these services in the light of experience, but an important addition was the provision of a bus service from 25 June 1913 between Abergele and Llanrwst via Llangerniew. Another new area to be opened-up was Anglesey where a bus service started on 13 July 1914 between Holyhead and Cemaes Bay. Other routes were planned but not introduced because of the deteriorating international situation which led to the outbreak of World War I on 1 August 1914 and by 13 April 1915 almost all bus services had ceased, except one between Betws-y-Coed, Penmachno and Cwm, which lasted until 14 April 1917.

The Great Western Railway operated a small group of bus services in the Wrexham area, together with others in the Bala, Oswestry, Corwen and Welshpool areas of central and mid Wales. They also operated along the coast between Aberystwyth and Aberaeron with links to a number of places, including Cardigan and New Quay, and there was a service from Aberystwyth to Borth. The Corris Railway and the Cambrian Railway were also involved in the business of early bus services in mid Wales. Those of the Corris Railway at Machynlleth passed to the GWR, then to Western Transport and, in due course, to Crosville.

Basically, the railway companies introduced bus services in order to enable more users to travel by rail. They were 'feeder' services, but as they evolved they naturally served local needs and it is important to appreciate the part they played in establishing the concept of bus services in many areas for which credit has been given to operators who, in reality, re-established 'war suspended' railway operated bus services. However, the Great Western Railway contrived to continue operating its buses and these were extensively developed in the twenties. Reference to their part in the establishment of Crosville, with the acquisition of the Western Transport Co Ltd, is referred to later in chapter 2.

Railway (Road Transport) Act 1928

Competition with the railways from the developing bus industry, and participation without strict authority in bus operation by certain railway companies, led to this Act becoming law on 3 August 1928. For a time nothing happened, except that in that month there had been a five per cent cut in the salaries and wages of Crosville's management and staff. Early in 1929 Crosville was quoted on the Stock Exchange at £1 6s 0d (£1.30) for each £1 share, and as a result of an approach by the LMSR Mr Claude and Mr W. J. Crosland-Taylor travelled to London for a meeting on 5 February 1929 with the railway company. At this time Crosville was one of the largest independent bus operators and at the meeting the discussion centred around the proposed offer to be made by the LMSR to all Crosville shareholders in order to buy out the concern. In the end the offer came to £1 7s 6d per share (£1.37½p) and after due consideration the Crosville Board decided to recommend acceptance of the offer; so from 1 May 1929 the Crosville belonged to the LMSR, which once again operated several of the bus services pioneered by the LNWR. However, the purchase brought the LMS up against the GWR bus services in north and mid Wales. The GWR desired an interest in Crosville, whereas the LMSR was interested in the Wrexham and District Transport Co.

How this situation was resolved, the effect of the Road Traffic Act of 1930, development in the thirties and eventual state ownership are matters which are considered in the following chapters.

2

Crosville in the Thirties

LMS Crosville

As recorded in the previous chapter, from 1 May 1929 Crosville became the property of the LMS, which decided to retain the goodwill attached to the name and for a year, until 1 May 1930, when a new company known as Crosville Motor Services Ltd was formed, the business was known as LMS Crosville. Some buses carried the LMS crest, but in due course an oval design was adopted with the words *LMS – Crosville* and the fleet number. The fleet colour became LMS maroon with cream relief (see chapter 8).

These years were of great importance because other negotiations were proceeding which were to have a profound effect on the future of Crosville. The first major event was related to negotiations between the various railway companies, the Tilling, and British Electric Traction groups, while the other was the acquisition by the LMS of three businesses in North Wales for merging with Crosville.

Holyhead Motors Company Ltd (Mona Maroon)

This operator had commenced bus services on Anglesey (its Welsh name being Mona) in the nineteen twenties and had developed a small group of routes radiating from Holyhead, whereas the trunk route between Holyhead and Bangor had been started by UNU (*see below*) of Caernarfon. By the time the business was purchased by the LMS for £26,500 it was owned by the Seaside Resorts & Developments Co Ltd, and in the opinion of the late W. J. Crosland-Taylor the LMS paid about five times its value. The buses were in a dreadful state, and there were huge stores of unsaleable spares which had been held in connection with the car side of the business. Conductors were paid 12s 6d (62½p) per week, and with annual takings running at £8,400 receipts were 5.1d (2p) per mile, with alleged costs of 4d (1½p) per mile without allowing for depreciation. However, Crosville was stuck with it and had to sort out the business which, of course, it did.

UNU (You need us!) of Caernarfon

As mentioned in the previous paragraph, this operator was a better proposition than Mona Maroon although it is suggested the business was worth about half of the £32,500 paid by the LMS. Established in the twenties UNU operated a number of strategic routes besides that from Bangor to Holyhead, insofar as they linked Caernarfon with Bangor, and Bangor with Llangefni. In addition UNU operated a service from Caernarfon to Birkenhead. Acquired by the LMS from a Mr W. Webster of Wigan on 1 January 1930, it still left a large number of small operators each with individual services which were mostly bought out by Crosville in the mid-thirties.

Brookes Bros of Rhyl

This was the most important of the three Welsh acquisitions, Rhyl being an important seaside resort with a substantial resident population centred at a strategic location in relation to Denbigh, St Asaph, Prestatyn, Abergele and numerous smaller settlements. It is believed that Brookes Bros (who traded as White Rose Motor Services) commenced as horsebus operators, initially used for tours originating from Rhyl, purchasing their first motor vehicle, a Lacre charabanc, in 1911. This was followed in 1912 by a small number of Leyland charabancs and two Leyland double-deckers for use on a town service at Rhyl.

Other routes were then developed with Brookes Bros' buses operating north to Holywell and Flint, east through Ruthin to Corwen and south to Abergele. Numerous other routes were operated within this general area, but Brookes Bros did not extend through Colwyn Bay to Llandudno which were linked to Rhyl by a service provided by the Llandudno Coaching Company. There is no record of any operating agreement as to spheres of influence, but the existence of such an arrangement seems very likely.

Development of the Brookes Bros' business had not been accompanied without competition – there was a particularly severe battle with Rhyl & Potteries Motors of Rhyl which eventually succumbed to Brookes Bros and Red Dragon of Denbigh. Brookes Bros had developed the use of the Shelvroke & Drewry toastrack for seasonal use in Rhyl (see chapter 8) and amongst the drivers in the twenties was one David Jones. So far as I can recollect he lived in the Ruthin area where he was the champion 'hedger and ditcher' and came to Rhyl in the summer to drive a toastrack. When the Brookes Bros' business was acquired by Crosville he carried on in the same way with his new employers and apart from the war years, continued to do so until the toastrack ceased operating in Rhyl in 1952. But when David Jones, by now in his late sixties, reported for employment the next year, he had to be shown how to drive a vehicle with normal gearbox. I was there at the time and it was decided to allocate him one of the Leyland TD5s which were very nice to drive. David could change-up alright and could manage changing-down from top to third, but could never master third to second. However he did a grand job, and I can remember him now, riding down Rhyl High Street on his Douglas motor cycle, still with carbide lamps, his Crosville 'issue dustcoat' flopping in the wind. He gave up bus driving in 1954 and another of the characters disappeared from the scene.

But to return to Brookes Bros. Negotiations were started by the LMS in 1929 and on 29 December 1929 a price based on assets plus goodwill was discussed – a figure approaching £250,000 was put forward. However, the LMS would not pay this, and although the railway company made a good offer it was not acceptable to Brookes Bros and the meeting broke up. In February 1930 there was a valuation of assets, with the result that the amount offered came down and in the end Brookes Bros agreed to sell for a price twenty two percent below the amount the LMS had offered to pay in the previous December, the business passing to Crosville on 1 May 1930, the same date as a new company was launched – Crosville Motor Services Ltd.

Crosville Motor Services Ltd

During the year since the LMS had purchased Crosville, negotiations had been proceeding between Thomas Tilling Ltd and the British Electric Traction Co Ltd, the result of which was an agreement whereby the bus companies would sell to the railway companies a number of shares in each bus company equal to that held by the largest shareholder. In some cases this meant half shares but in no case did it mean control. To further complicate matters Tilling, which had originated in London and was seeking outlets for expansion outside London, came to an agreement with the British Automobile Traction Co (a BET subsidiary) which resulted in 1928 in a new company, Tilling & British Automobile Traction Ltd, being formed. Meanwhile, each of the two groups had separately obtained a controlling interest in certain bus undertakings so that the pattern of ownership which emerged was either Tilling, or BET, or joint Tilling & British Automobile Traction.

An important clause in the agreement between the railways and the bus holding company groups was that the latter were to be responsible for the operating of the bus companies and the railways would have suitable representation on the boards of directors, the chairman in each case to be appointed by the bus groups. In the case of Crosville the business was put into the pool by the LMS which sold half of its interest to Tilling and British Automobile Traction. The first directors of the new company were W. S. Wreathall, chairman, G. Cardwell, C. D. Stanley, Ashton Davies, O. Glynne Roberts and Claude Crosland-Taylor,

29

the last three representing the LMS. In addition to representation on the boards of directors it was further arranged that for each of the companies concerned there should be a standing joint committee which would set about to devise ways and means of co-ordination between the railways and the bus companies. These committees, which still exist, have done a great deal of useful work over the years.

Road Traffic Act 1930

By 1927 the road passenger transport industry had reached a turning point insofar as the days of competition had reached a critical position and it was obvious that the government was going to impose some form of control in the interests of road safety and the general stabilisation of an industry which had grown far faster than anyone anticipated. The vehicles had improved and developed with the introduction of pneumatic tyres and other refinements, to the point where the term 'luxury coach' could rightly be employed, and long-distance services were poised for a rapid and dramatic expansion. In 1928 a Royal Commission on transport was set up and in due course recommended in respect of road passenger transport:

(a) the licensing of vehicles, to ensure that they came up to a proper standard of repair and maintenance,
(b) the licensing of drivers, and conductors to ensure adequate standards of behaviour on the roads,
(c) the licensing of services, including timetables and faretables, to obviate unfair competition and ensure that a reliable standard of service was provided for the travelling public.

All these recommendations were embodied in the Road Traffic Act which became effective on 1 August 1930, and which also provided for the setting-up of traffic areas with Traffic Commissioners to administer licensing provisions. The North Western traffic area, administered from Manchester, covers most of the area in which Crosville operate, although some services fall within the jurisdiction of the South Wales and the

West Midlands traffic areas. The physical strife between rival operators on the roads was now transferred to legal strife in the Traffic Commissioners' courts and the road service licence became a vital document without which a bus service could not be provided. When the Road Traffic Act became law in 1930 Crosville arranged a series of lectures for its management staff on the provisions of the new Act, and then established its licensing department. It took three weeks for Crosville to prepare its applications and a small lorry was required to convey the documents to the Traffic Commissioners' offices in Manchester. Crosville, and the industry in general, welcomed the 1930 Act and could now develop its business without being told one morning that someone had got a bus and was pirating one of its best routes. The licensing regulations changed the situation in regard to the purchase of businesses, the important point being that an operator could not, and cannot, purchase another operator's licences. The purchaser can pay for the assets and goodwill but must apply for the licences, to which there can be objections by statutory objectors. In general most 'takeovers' go through, but instances where there have been attempts to 're-introduce' dormant excursion and tour licences have resulted in the applications being refused.

The new licensing scheme came into force on 9 February 1931 and Crosville purchased several businesses between its re-organisation in May 1930 and that date, the most important being W. Edwards (Red Dragon) of Denbigh on 31 July 1930 and the North Wales Silver Motors Ltd on 1 August 1930. The fact that most of the businesses were with some notable exceptions small, may have arisen from the inability to continue of many small operators whose vehicles could not comply with the regulations set out in the Road Traffic Act 1930. The Llandudno Coaching & Carriage Co Ltd (with whom there had been a joint LMS and Tilling/BAT agreement since 28 December 1929) was acquired on 1 November 1930 and during the next five years a large number of bus operators in Wales were acquired, the most important being the Western Transport Co Ltd on 1 May 1933.

North Wales Silver Motors Ltd

This business was established in 1911 as the Llandudno Automobile Touring Co Ltd with a capital of £18,000, and by 1913 it was operating to Penmaenmawr, subsequently extending this service to Llanfairfechan. This became the North Wales Silver Motors Ltd in 1914 which in 1916 commenced a service to Llanrwst. During World War I the company served Kinmel Camp, an interesting situation because the camp is much nearer to Rhyl than Llandudno where the Mostyn Broadway depot (now closed) was established by this firm, which at the time of its sale to Crosville was operating 31 buses.

Llandudno Coaching and Carriage Co Ltd (Royal Blue)

This company developed from a horse-drawn coach business, having as its base the premises which became Crosville's Oxford Road depot at Llandudno (closed June 1971). At one time it could boast the ownership of 150 horses, some of which were used to work a horse-drawn stage service from the Gogarth Abbey Hotel via the Promenade to the Little Orme. In 1912 it was operating from Llandudno pier to Pennhynside for 2d (1p). In 1918 all the horses and related equipment were sold and motor vehicles introduced. During 1923 the British Automobile Traction Co Ltd acquired the major holding in the Llandudno Coaching Co., with Mr W. S. Wreathall as chairman. The Bangor Blue company was acquired in 1928 and fierce competition resulted with UNU, which caused the former considerable difficulties as it was facing heavy competition in the Llandudno area from the North Wales Silver Motors and the Llandudno & Colwyn Bay Electric Railway Co Ltd.

North Wales re-organisation

The acquisition by Crosville of all these businesses meant that it had consolidated bus operating on the North Wales coast. The company was able to re-organise and rationalise the services and bus workings in the area concerned in order to find the best methods of working. Average speeds varied from one service to another, even in the same area, some services being too fast whilst others were desperately slow. Different methods of duty schedules were in operation, while there were no reliable statistics on which to judge performance. One of the principal items of expenditure in bus operation is the wages of drivers and conductors, and the most important statistic the ratio between hours paid and hours actually worked when the wheels are turning. During 1930 and 1931 Crosville managed to increase the average running speed to 15mph (including intermediate stops) and obtained an operating efficiency whereby out of every 100 hours paid, some 80 hours were wheel-turning time.

Although traffic receipts were increasing each year at this time, (as were the miles, passengers and profits) the receipts per mile declined. The dilemma was whether or not to increase mileage in order to decrease costs per mile, or cut out some poor mileage, which would probably increase the receipts per mile.

On top of the new ownership and acquisitions, a board decision was taken in February 1932 to the effect that the Western Transport Co of Wrexham should be amalgamated with Crosville, this taking place on 1 May 1933. It was a very important acquisition by Crosville, the biggest that it had undertaken in terms of vehicles, even allowing for the merger with part of the North Western Road Car Co Ltd nearly forty years later in 1972.

Western Transport Co Ltd

The original company was the Wrexham Tramways Ltd which opened the line for traffic from Wrexham to Johnstown (a distance of $3\frac{1}{4}$ miles) in October 1876, the line subsequently being extended to Rhosllanerchrugog. At that time it was worked by horses. In due course the Wrexham Tramways Ltd sold out to the Drake & Gorham Electric Power and Traction Co Ltd, which on 10 December 1898 gave notice under the Tramways Act 1870 that it proposed to replace the horse operation with electric traction. However, it soon withdrew in favour of the British Electric Traction Co Ltd, which promoted the Wrexham & District Electric Tramways Co Ltd. Electrification was carried out by Dick Kerr & Co Ltd. An extension was authorised from Johnstown (where the tram depot and offices of the company were located) to Ruabon, but this was never built. The new electrified tramway was opened on 4 April 1903, and in 1913 bus operation was commenced as 'feeders' to the trams. After World War I further bus services were introduced, but the company established a policy of routing the buses via the main roads, which allowed competitors to introduce successful alternative bus services. Amongst the tramways' competitors was the Great Western Railway. The result was a foregone conclusion, the tramway being closed on 31 March 1927. In 1930 the GWR bus services were merged with those of the tramway company and a new company was formed named the Western Transport Co Ltd.

However, the new company was still relatively small and there was no possibility of paying a dividend, so it was arranged for it to be merged with Crosville on 1 May 1933, by an exchange of 155,000 Western Transport shares for 155,000 Crosville shares – in the view of the late W. J. Crosland-Taylor a bargain for the Western Transport shareholders.

In its heyday the tramway company owned ten open-top double-deck cars which maintained a service that provided for the first departure from Rhos at 0450, then half-hourly until 0940, and approximately every fifteen minutes until 2100, then 2140, and 2224. Trams returned from Wrexham at 0520 and half-hourly until 1020, every fifteen minutes until 2100, then half-hourly until 2300. Sunday service was less frequent. Fares were: Rhos to Wrexham 4d single (2p) 6d return (2½p); Rhostyllen to Wrexham 2d single (1p) 3d return (1½p); Rhos to Wrexham weekly ticket 2/2d (11p).

Above: Leyland coach No 774 in the 1930s' coach livery. (*Crosville*)

Below: Three rebodied Ks, including K32 and 33 on a private hire in 1937. (*Crosville*)

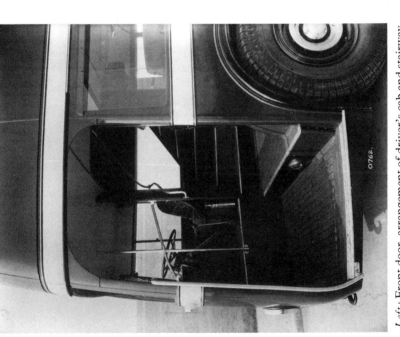

Left: Front door, arrangement of driver's cab and stairway of AEC Q No 1000 (later L87 then L68) as new in 1933. (*Crosville*)

Right: Pre-Second World War timetable display frames. (*Crosville*)

Competition with independent operators

At the time when Crosville took over the operations of the
Western Transport Company, there were numerous independent
operators in the Wrexham and Oswestry areas. Almost every
main Western Transport route was covered either in whole or
part by one or more independant. Relations had not been good
between these independent operators and Western Transport;
there were constant complaints by them that the company's
buses were holding back and infringing on their times unfairly to
secure passengers. Dealing with this was difficult, as prior to the
introduction of the Road Traffic Act drivers had been actively
encouraged in this practice, whereas after the introduction of the
Act it became illegal and it was difficult to persuade staff that
what the company had previously regarded as meritorious must
now be regarded as reprehensible.

Western Transport operating practices were found to be
wasteful by Crosville standards, many more buses being
employed than would be necessary with economically arranged
timetables. In starting to put this to rights in order to reduce
costs to a level comparable with those in the rest of the system,
Crosville decided that there must be wholesale revision of
timetables. To do this the goodwill and agreement of the
independents had to be secured.

The independents in the Wrexham area were banded into an
association, the secretary of which was a man named Tooth
(who, incidentally, was a body-builder who constructed a few
bodies on Leyland Cub and LT5A chassis (see chapter 7) for
Crosville). Claude Crosland-Taylor saw that much advantage
could be obtained if Crosville were to become a member of the
association. Consequently he applied for membership on behalf
of the company, offering to pay a considerably enhanced
membership fee to represent the number of vehicles operated by
the company in the area, and this was accepted.

After the company had joined, the local officials regularly
attended the meetings of the association which were held in a
smoke-filled room at a public house near the Brook Street bus

terminus in Wrexham. These meetings were sometimes very stormy and no punches were pulled in arguing about infringement of times and similar matters. However, there were hammered out many agreements for changes which brought benefits both to the company and the independent operators and better services for the travelling public.

The 'main line', as it was colloquially called, provided a good example of the problem involved. This was the old tramway route between Wrexham and Rhosllanerchrugog via Johnstown. In addition to Crosville, which was running a quarter-hourly service, there were four other operators on the through route: Williams of Ponciau; Phillips of Rhostyllen; Wrights of Penycae; and Owen of Rhostyllen. Additionally the section between Johnstown and Wrexham was covered by two other Crosville services (that between Wrexham and Oswestry and that between Wrexham and Llangollen) and by that of another operator, Meredith & Jesson, which ran between Wrexham and Ruabon. The result was a total frequency of a bus less than every five minutes between Johnstown and Wrexham. The existing timetables provided for excessive lay-over times at the terminal points, and Crosville saw that if this could be reduced it would be able to maintain the same level of service with one bus fewer, a very valuable saving, as to man a bus all day required at least three drivers and three conductors. To negotiate the necessary change in times and reconcile them with all the other operators was obviously no easy matter with such close frequencies. It is to the credit of all concerned that agreement was reached and the revised timetables introduced in 1934 lasted at least into the nineteen seventies.

This problem was present, to some extent, on almost all other routes but Crosville's policy paid off and many similar agreements were reached. Some of the major independants saw the advantage of selling-out to Crosville and there were numerous acquisitions by the company in that area between 1933, when the merger with Western Transport took place, and the outbreak of war in 1939. These acquisitions included: Rothwell of Holt, Reeves, Tylor, Plate, and Jones (all of

Oswestry), J. Price of Wrexham, Roberts of Southsea, Williams of Pentre Broughton, and many others. The merger solved the GWR/LMS problem over participation in Crosville, because the new financial structure gave the GWR a $12\frac{1}{2}$ per cent holding in Crosville as against $37\frac{1}{2}$ per cent held by the LMS.

One-man operation in North Wales

On account of the need to hold down operating costs in North Wales and to cope with the weight restrictions on the Menai Bridge, Crosville made extensive use of one-man buses in Bangor, Anglesey and other parts of North Wales. This accounted for the large intake of Leyland Cubs from 1932 to 1935. Most of these were the usual driver-behind-engine, 20- and 26-seater types, which were quite adequate for the majority of routes on Anglesey and elsewhere. For the main Bangor – Holyhead service a batch of forward-drive, 31-seater Cubs was purchased in 1934/5, replacing the SOS Q-types, which prior to that had been the only vehicles in the fleet capable of complying with the Menai Bridge weight restriction. The forward-drive Cubs, of course, carried conductors. One-man operation on the others was very economical, as one-man operators were only paid a pittance over normal driving rate. At one time the addition was as little as $1\frac{1}{2}$d (1p) per hour. No ticket machines were fitted and the driver sat at the wheel, with cash bag and ticket punch slung over his shoulder and a large ticket rack in a box at his right-hand side.

Railway 'loaned staff'

Arising from the merger the GWR bus interests referred to above and those which took place with Crosville at Corwen, Oswestry, Pwllheli, Aberystwyth, Machynlleth and Dolgellau, Crosville had a number of former GWR staff in its employ. They were known as 'loaned staff' and belonged to the National Union of Railwaymen, whereas Crosville staff were in general members of the Transport & General Workers' Union. The 'loaned staff' retained railway rates of pay and certain railway privileges as regards coal, free travel and other matters. This caused constant friction, and negotiations took place whereby cash compensation would be paid to the NUR men in return for which they would renounce their rights and become members of the T&GWU, working under the same terms and conditions as the other staff. All the staff signed and accepted the arrangement on 1 August 1933, with the exception of an inspector at Aberystwyth.

Llandudno & Colwyn Bay Electric Railway Co Ltd

Crosville was also in competition with another tramway in North Wales, the Llandudno & Colwyn Bay Electric Railway Co. Ltd. This undertaking opened for traffic on 19 October 1907 and as its title implies, operated between Llandudno and Colwyn Bay. The route was via Rhos-on-Sea and until 21 September 1930 operated to the Queens Hotel, Old Colwyn, after which date the system terminated at Greenfield Road, Colwyn Bay. During the late 1920s the tramway company proposed operating buses within the area of Colwyn Bay but nothing came of the scheme. The proposals may well have been in competition with Colwyn Bay UDC which in 1928 obtained a 'general powers' Act of Parliament including authority to run buses, which it still does in the summer, from Rhos-on-Sea Pier via the Promenade to the junction with Beach Road, Old Colwyn and to Colwyn Bay Zoo.

Claude Crosland-Taylor

The momentum of the early thirties was overshadowed by the untimely death on 31 March 1935 of Claude Crosland-Taylor. Aged 45 years he had been unwell for several years but he had guided the Crosville for 24 years and when he died he was the managing director of England's third largest provincial bus company. As a result of his death his younger brother, W. J. Crosland-Taylor became acting manager and he was appointed to the post of general manager in the same year. When he retired in 1958 the family involvement with Crosville came to an end.

He was succeeded by Bernard Griffiths, the General Manager of
United Welsh Services Limited, Swansea.

Development of express services

As mentioned in the previous chapter, Crosville had commenced
a Liverpool–London service in the late twenties but was in
competition with Pearson, Jones & Horn (who operated a
Southport – Liverpool – London service) whose business was
purchased in 1936 by Crosville and Ribble. Crosville took the
Liverpool – London service which was consolidated with the
existing operations, and after trying several alternative routes
finally settled for a route from Liverpool (Pier Head) via
Birmingham, Stratford-on-Avon and Oxford to London
(Victoria Coach Station) where a Crosville inspector was based.
Charting for the service was carried out at Liverpool and
London and conductors were not employed, the drivers
collecting tickets.

The usual proceedure on Crosville express services was for the
passenger to apply in advance for a seat, returning to the office to
purchase the ticket once the availability of the seat was
confirmed. A booking reference number was entered on the
ticket and upon boarding the coach the conductor issued an
ordinary bell punch ticket in exchange to the value of the single
fare, or 50% of the return fare. In post World War II days this
system was upheld by the issue of 'exchange tickets' purchased
for the face value. This practice changed again so that a 'tear-off'
portion of the ticket was returned to the passenger and, of
course, the reservation system has changed, with most services
offering a 'walk-on' booking system. A number of express
services from the Wrexham area to Rhyl, Llandudno, Blackpool
and Birkenhead had been added by the acquisition of the
Western Transport Co Ltd. Services from Newcastle-under-
Lyme via Crewe to Blackpool and Llandudno had been added in
1931, a Warrington to Rhyl service was commenced in 1938 and
the last development before World War II was the introduction
in 1939 of a service from Caernarfon to Aberystwyth.

North Staffordshire Road Transport Bill

Early in 1937 the City of Stoke-on-Trent promoted the North Staffordshire Road Transport Bill under which all the operators in the Potteries would be combined into a transport board. Naturally all the operators, including Crosville, opposed the Bill, this time from the Omnibus Owners' Association, and as a result of the opposition the Bill was rejected at the second reading.

War Shadows

In the late 1930s the possibility of war with Germany became more likely with each passing year and it became a race against time to get as many improvements as possible completed before war was declared. During 1938 W. J. Crosland-Taylor became a member of the Chairmen of the North Western Traffic Commissioners advisory committee, but the crisis of that year passed and he was on holiday in France in August 1939, returning just as the evacuation of children from large towns was commencing on 1 September 1939. His family crossed from France on the night of 1/2 September, and on 3 September 1939 war was declared.

3

World War II

War with Germany was declared on 3 September 1939 and in those first weeks business was much as usual, although a number of the staff who were service reservists had left to join their units, while on 21 September 1939 the chairman Mr W. S. Wreathall died, his place being taken by Mr J. S. Wills. Petrol rationing was introduced in the September and service mileage was reduced by 20%, although work services were retained at their normal level. Later in the war evening services were much reduced due to the risk of air raids and the fact that most evening entertainments ceased. Traffic started to increase for a number of reasons: evacuees being visited by parents, servicemen travelling to and from their units, and the gradual involvement of the civilian population in civil defence and other wartime activities, besides the restlessness of a people whose future was uncertain. October 1939 saw the limit on standing passengers raised from five to eight and later this was increased to twelve.

As time went on the company was faced with new regulations which affected many of its activities, in fact the government was publishing statutory rules and orders at the rate of 2,000 per year, each one of which had the effect of an Act of Parliament. Buses were the subject of reduced headlights and interior lights, the lifeguard's wing and platform edges being painted white as an aid in the blackout. A number of single-deck buses were converted into ambulances, whilst others had their interiors re-arranged to increase the seating capacity. Amongst the statutory rules and orders were instructions on how to immobilise buses, but at the same time as all these additional operating problems were introduced there were calls for extra buses and new services to feed the factories which were engaging hundreds of workers in order to work around the clock.

An interesting innovation in Crewe at this time was the establishment of a committee consisting of local Crosville management, local trade union representatives from the Rolls Royce factory (then making aero-engines), and the LMS railway works (then making tanks). This committee met regularly and was most effective in dealing with complaints and suggestions about bus services, which would have been most difficult to handle and co-ordinate otherwise. Many employers accepted the need to stagger hours in order to economise in the number of buses used, which not only meant a saving in costs but reduced the use of scarce fuel and manpower. However, many additional vehicles had to be 'hired in' to meet the demand. On 22 October 1941 Crosville was scheduled under the Essential Work Order which, in theory, meant that no employee could leave without special permission, but many managed to get around the regulations. Of course many men joined the armed forces as volunteers or through conscription, and their places were taken by older people who came out of retirement, and by conductresses.

Conductresses

The first conductresses were engaged in April 1940 and were placed under the direction of a lady supervisor who interviewed almost every female applicant despite the travelling involved between depots, the larger of which in due course had forewomen where several conductresses were employed. It is perhaps not generally realised that during the war younger women not suitably employed had to join the armed forces or the Women's Land Army, or take up employment in a firm stipulated under the Essential Work Order, such as transport, industry, or the medical profession.

Air raids and requisitioning of bus depots

Merseyside was heavily bombed on several occasions and although many employees suffered great personal hardship arising from actual damage to their own houses, they made considerable efforts which resulted in a high standard of bus service reliability. To their own problems was added damage to buses and depots, both Rock Ferry and Edge Lane depots being involved in air raid damage. Oswestry depot was requisitioned early in 1941 by the Ministry of Aircraft Production and part of Bangor depot was taken-over by Daimler before the Regional Transport Commissioners were able to point out that without buses to transport the workers the factories would not function. Reason prevailed and no more bus depots were taken over – although it was 'touch and go' for a while.

The threat of air raids resulted in the dispersal of government offices besides factories and this placed a burden on the existing bus services which were planned for quite different levels of traffic. North Wales is a good example insofar as in normal times there was a reasonable standard of service to the coastal resorts and the immediate hinterland, the winter service being heavily supplemented in the summer. To this area came the Inland Revenue, which took over most of Llandudno's hotels, while to Llandrillo-yn-Rhos (near Colwyn Bay) came the Ministry of Food. Bangor theatre and the Grand Theatre at Llandudno were used for broadcasting and in 1943 Crosville took part in a programme in the *Bridge Builder* series that was relayed later to the United States. Added to the re-location of government departments was the establishment of airfields and military encampments. Amongst many which sprang up, both big and small, were Royal Air Force stations at Valley, Harwarden and Sealand and an American hospital at Llandudno. Bus drivers had to look out for tanks, self-propelled guns and other items of military hardware being manoeuvred on the narrow roads in Wales. There was much additional passenger traffic together with heavier road use, much of it in an area unaccustomed to such activity.

Wartime operating problems

Some people still managed to have their summer holidays and as there were no express coach services they had little alternative but to travel by rail despite exhortations which asked 'IS YOUR JOURNEY REALLY NECESSARY?'. But perhaps the strains of war made some such journeys necessary, if only to escape from cities subject to air raids. This placed a burden on the bus services and there was no scope for duplicates to cater for last-minute overloads. The 21.05 from Caernarfon to Llandudno was the last through journey on a service worked by 32-seater KAs. The trick was to join it at Caernarfon depot or thereabouts on its inward journey to Caernarfon Square and hope that the conductor would let you stay on at the terminal. Aber Falls was a popular attraction and it was not unusual to wait for two or three full buses to pass before managing to board – this on a service with a 20-minute frequency. But this was by no means unusual and the last buses from Rhyl, Chester and other centres were all in the same situation. Another privation of war was rationing; it brought problems but it developed business for the buses because people would travel out to the countryside to purchase eggs, strawberries, mushrooms or other produce, direct from farms. Other enthusiasts went out blackberrying and there was a great deal more walking and rambling than takes place today. Clothes were on ration and everyone had an allocation of coupons. The issue of uniforms was no exception and represented twelve coupons per annum for a full outfit out of the then total of sixty-six. Other wartime measures involved the employment of women in the workshops, and to help the national campaign to save fuel producer-gas trailers were introduced as described in chapter 8.

Under Tilling control

Even the war did not bring a halt to the slowly evolving pattern of the bus industry. In 1942 it was agreed to end the agreement between Tillings' and the BET whereby there had been joint control of subsidiaries through the T&BAT organisation and to share out the companies involved between the two holding concerns. As a result on 3 December 1942 Crosville became a Tilling subsidiary with Sir J. Frederick Heaton replacing Mr J. S. Wills as chairman of the company. Tilling control brought a change in emphasis in a number of directions, including advertising on buses, investment in property, but perhaps the most obvious change so far as the public and staff were concerned was the change of livery from maroon to green.

Utility buses

Details of buses acquired during World War II are set out in chapter 8, and apart from a few 'unfrozen' Leylands consisted for the most part of Guys and Bristols. With the change to Tilling control the Bristol chassis has featured prominently in the Crosville fleet since the war, and Bristol chassis are still being taken into stock under National Bus Company control.

Anglesey

The spring of 1945 brought an awareness to the British public that it was very likely that the war would soon be over – at least in Europe – and it was in this atmosphere of hope that Crosville organised a celebration luncheon to mark the inauguration of double-deck buses into Anglesey, which is linked to the mainland near Bangor by a road suspension bridge over the Menai Straits. Built in 1826 by Thomas Telford, there was a weight restriction of 4 tons 5 cwt, and specially-built lightweight 20-seaters had to be used. One night shortly before the war, the bridge was damaged during a particularly severe westerly gale, when the holding bolts on the Caernarfonshire side snapped. Although temporary repairs were carried out, it was necessary to reconstruct the bridge in steel in place of the original iron structure. This work was undertaken during the war with no cessation of traffic. When rebuilt the weight restriction and toll was removed on 31 December 1940 and Crosville's first double-decker across the bridge in 1945 was M88. Conwy bridge was also a problem for similar reasons, although conventional single-deckers could be used. This bridge, its rebuilding, and the effect on the Crosville services is described in chapter 4.

End of the war

With the end of the war in Europe in May 1945 and in the Far East in August 1945 there was some restoration of services and mileage, to be soon followed by private parties and tours, with a boom in traffic of all kinds in 1946. The return of peace was celebrated by street parties and similar events, and I can remember K1, together with another similar coach, resplendent in their pre-war coach livery of grey, green and cream, picking us up and taking us out for the first private hire that I can recall. Then there was the restoration of express services, and a first memorable ride on the coach from Llandudno to the awesome spectacle of Liverpool, still devastated from the war. In June 1946 there was a victory parade in London. After the celebrations there was much work to do in order to put Crosville back to rights. At the same time there was the prospect of State control, so the future was open to question.

4

Developments in the forties and fifties

Post-war restoration of bus services

Irrespective of the political outlook, Crosville began in earnest
the long hard task of recovering from the ravages of war. Staff
were returning from the armed forces, requisitioned buildings
were being released, there was a full programme of renewals and
improvements to premises, and the first service restorations took
place in 1945. However, the aftermath of war brought its
industrial problems, and in 1947 there were a number of
unofficial strikes regarding conditions of employment. Work
stopped at all the English depots except Liverpool, but at only
two Welsh depots, Mold and Flint. On the bright side, the first
new post-war buses began to arrive from the manufacturers, but
there was a long way to go and to assist in meeting the rapidly-
expanding traffic, numerous second-hand buses were also
purchased in this period.

Transport Act 1947

By virtue of this Act the then newly-formed British Transport
Commission was empowered to acquire bus companies, but
straightforward nationalisation, as for instance with the
railways, was not part of the Act and did not take place. It
should, however, be appreciated that the railways had
substantial financial interests (amounting to some 45%) in the
bus companies concerned, although this interest appears to have
been somewhat higher in Tilling group companies than in the

BET-owned bus companies. Negotiations took place on the basis of valuation laid down in the Act, namely, physical assets plus a certain number of years' profit as a goodwill item.

The 1947 Act did, however, contemplate 'permissively', 'area schemes' of nationalisation by which the buses would be brought under the control of regional boards responsible to the British Transport Commission. Ownership of one of the two large groups of provincial bus companies was presumably seen as a means of achieving this end by virtue of having a company already established in each area on which to create an 'area scheme'. The one 'area scheme' for which active planning commenced was in the north-east of England, but so strong was the opposition that it did not come to fruition. In September 1948 Thomas Tilling Ltd agreed to sell its interest in the bus companies on 1 January 1949, and the British Transport Commission acquired through the machinery of the Companies Act the share capital of the companies involved during the year ending 31 December 1949. Although the BTC became owners of virtually the entire share capital and appointed the directors, the structure of management remained unchanged. Crosville Motor Services Ltd, in common with other Tilling companies, retained its title and the Tilling Group Management Board continued to control the overall policy of the company.

Under British Transport Commission control

As a result of the BTC acquisition Sir Frederick Heaton retired as chairman, and in March 1949 his place was taken by Mr F. P. Arnold. At the same time Mr W. J. Crosland-Taylor was appointed a director in accordance with the BTC decision to make general managers members of their companies' boards. In the meantime Mr P. G. Stone Clarke acted as chairman. Originally an engineer, he became general manager of the Western and Southern National Omnibus Companies but left the Tilling Group to take up an appointment with the British Electric Traction Co Ltd.

So far as Crosville was concerned 549,428 ordinary £1 shares were transferred to the British Transport Commission, which paid £4 8s 9d (£4.47p) each for them. The BTC already owned the railway holdings and in due course purchased the remainder from private holdings. As the capital of Crosville at that time was £1,100,000 in £1 shares, it would seem that at the price paid per share by the BTC the company was worth £4,881,250.

Post-war private hire, excursions and tours

There was a heavy demand for private hire in the years immediately following the war but fuel was severely restricted in 1948. The 12½ percent mileage cut on private hire remained in 1949, and it was not until 1950 that fuel became generally available. Crosville had, however, re-introduced excursions and tours, and in order to cover the work a number of 20-seater Leyland Cubs was painted in the post-war coach livery. An extremely interesting introduction was the use of two SOS charabancs, numbered Q1 and Q2. These were allocated to Llandudno Town depot, as were the first new Bedford SLs. To supplement further the coach fleet at this time, new Bristol L types working into Llandudno as express services were also used on tours. The Leyland Tiger coaches were still scarce and remained the 'flagships' of the coach fleet at that time. Crosville has always referred to its excursions and tours as 'SSBs' – single-seat bookings.

Christmas 1948

Late in 1948 Crosville had to decide whether to run Sunday services on Christmas Day, or whether to operate special services for essential workers and hospital visiting. Working on Christmas Day is unpopular, it is costly, there is little revenue and if special timetables are operated the public tend to be unaware of what is actually being provided. In the end a momentous decision was taken and Crosville advertised 'no service on Christmas Day'.

Post-war development of express services

The Festival of Britain took place in the summer of 1951 on the South Bank, Waterloo and at Battersea Gardens, London. It was a major event and to cater for the expected increase in traffic Crosville applied for and was granted permission to operate its August duplication on the Liverpool–London service during the period of the Festival. At the same time, McShane's applied for a Liverpool–London service. Crosville objected, particularly as it had paid a large sum in the thirties for the goodwill of McShane's Liverpool–London service. As a result, Crosville came to an agreement with the railways that Crosville should apply for unlimited duplication from 1 May 1951. In the event both trains and coaches ran fully loaded but after the event Crosville reverted to the duplication allowance.

Rhyl, Llandudno and the other North Wales resorts were very popular in Merseyside, with the result that Crosville's express services were hard pressed to cater for the traffic, particularly at peak summer weekends. In order to provide the necessary vehicles large numbers of double-deck buses were hired from Liverpool, Birkenhead, Wallasey, Widnes and Warrington corporations. The principal provider of these vehicles was Liverpool Corporation, to such an extent that the route service number (127) and terminal destinations were included on the destination indicators of the buses regularly involved. Upon arrival at Rhyl they were parked in rows, company by company, at the Albion Works yard. The coastal resorts were, of course, served by numerous operators including Midland Red and many others. On busy Saturdays the bus stations were crowded with a wide variety of buses and coaches, including the unusual rear-entrance, underfloor-engine Atkinsons of North Western.

Fares applications

The post-war boom in traffic coupled with increased frequencies on many services led to a reduction occurring during the first half of 1948 in receipts per bus mile which were then in the

Above: Leyland TD4 with ECW body at Colwyn Bay. (*C. Shears*)

Below: The aftermath of the fire at Rhyl in July 1945. (*Crosville*)

Above: P27 a 1937 Leyland Cub with Brush 26 seat body (with war-time white edges to the mudguards) stands in the entrance to Corwen depot. (*Crosville*)

Below: Denbigh depot with KA bus and KA coach. Note the staff, some of whom are wearing winter, and others summer, uniforms. (*Crosville*)

region of 8d to 9d (4p) per mile. It should be appreciated that fares were still at pre-war levels and there was pressure from all quarters to provide additional services together with increased frequencies. To a large extent services were improved, particularly in the summer season, and in many cases the number of journeys provided exceeded those operated in 1939, although in some areas not all the pre-war mileage had been restored.

Another method of providing the increased capacity was to get as many routes as possible authorised for double-deck operation so that the need could be matched without the having to increase the number of buses required.

Inflation is not a new word, nor is it a new experience, and between the end of World War II and the end of 1950 wage awards alone had cost Crosville an additional half-million pounds in addition to those given during the war, for which the estimated annual cost amounted to approximately £300,000 per annum. To add to the misery was a 9d (4p) per gallon tax on diesel and petrol in the April 1950 budget which added a further £150,000 to the operating costs. Whilst economies were being made by a change over from petrol to diesel engines, and reductions in clerical staff arising from the introduction of ticket machines, it was clear that an increase in fares could not be avoided. Crosville's first increase in fares was implemented in 1950, but only applied to Crewe town services, the first general increase being implemented in February 1951. Because of the length of time it took for the application to be considered, and in due course granted, a second application was made and implemented in August 1951. Since then fares applications have become an annual event, and it is an unfortunate sign of the times that rapidly increasing costs and reductions in the number of persons wishing to use the buses has resulted, on occasions, in the instances when more than one increase in fares has occurred in a period of twelve months.

'Bell punch' tickets

Bus services are not 'big business' – they exist on a multitude of small transactions which combine to produce the revenues, and the best method of collecting this money and of securing it against pilferage, has always taken up a large proportion of the bus manager's time. Until the nineteen fifties Crosville used the 'bell punch system' for fare collection. The usual practice was the employment of a separate conductor on each vehicle, who walked up and down collecting fares and issuing pre-priced tickets from a rack, which he clipped in the stage name or number at which the passenger boarded with a bell punch giving a distinctive ring.

Tickets went through a process of evolution and development as did all other aspects of running buses and in the early days separate single and return tickets were issued, the passenger on the return journey receiving an exchange ticket of equivalent fare value. These early tickets were headed

but in due course the word 'Grey' was dropped. Later the tickets were re-styled insofar as the same ticket was issued for both single and return journeys. In this situation a passenger tendering a return ticket had the top half removed and was issued with an exchange ticket. These tickets were in three different colours, blue, pink and white, and showed a range of fares on each side, the conductor being required to punch the appropriate fare. Later still, probably as a war-time economy measure, white tickets with two diagonal red stripes and endorsed 'no fare value' were issued in exchange for return tickets.

During the war a number of 'low value' single tickets came into use and for a time these were 'miniaturised' to save paper, to a vertical size roughly two-thirds of a standard 'bell punch' ticket. Another war-time economy was the 'marrying-up' of different values to equate with the fare paid. 'Bell punch' tickets to the value of £1 5s 0d (£1.25p) existed, at first in $\frac{1}{2}$d denominations, then in 1d intervals, reducing to 3d, and in the higher value the different tickets were issued at 6d (2$\frac{1}{2}$p) intervals.

Weekly, season, and multi-part 'bell punch' tickets were issued – the latter were issued for a wide range of specially linked connecting journeys in West Wales. In the Wirral a series of single tickets with fare stages overprinted were available.

Conductors were issued with two boxes, and while one was in use the 'X' box was being checked in the ticket office. Stocks of tickets were held at all depots in a range of denominations to cover the services operated from that depot. Bulk stock of tickets was held at Chester and the ordering, distributing and manual checking of tickets and ticket boxes was a monumental task, involving the employment of a large number of clerical staff.

Ticket machines

After some unsatisfactory pre-war experiments at Chester and Wrexham with Setright, TIM, and Willebrew machines, Crosville gave the matter further consideration after World War II, and in January 1949 introduced Setright speed models at Liverpool and Warrington depots. In the same year experiments were carried out with 'Ultimate' ticket machines at Llandudno Junction, Crewe and a number of other locations, but their range of issue was insufficient for Crosville. In 1949 a new Setright machine cost £45 and it could (and still can!) print and issue a wide range of different types of tickets, add up its sales, and record a number of other useful pieces of statistical information. The ticket box was much smaller, and the office work involved is only a fraction of that required with the labour-intensive 'bell punch' system. Crosville placed an order for 200 Setright machines in May 1949 with the result that Crewe was converted in October 1950, followed by Liverpool, Chester, Wrexham, Birkenhead and Runcorn during 1951, and over the next two years all depots were converted. At the present time the

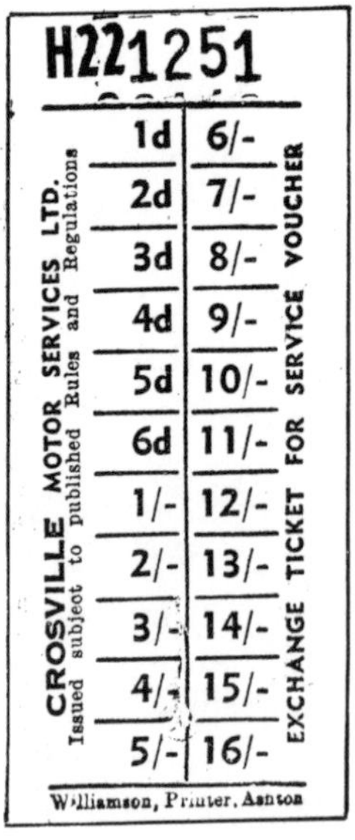

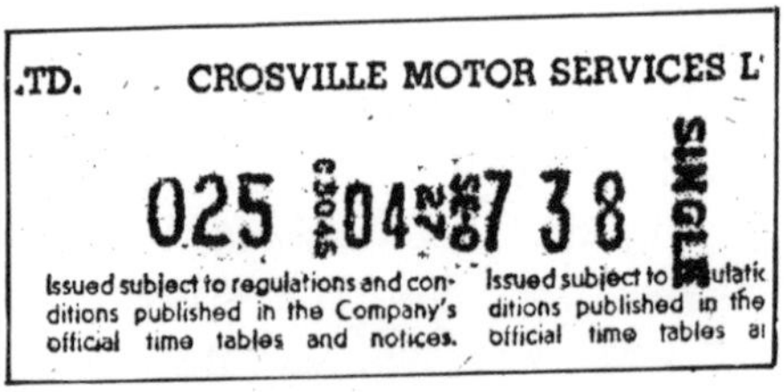

Top left ticket:

Crosville Motor Services Limited

A | BY SEA | **C**

LLANDUDNO to DOUGLAS
AND RETURN
**TO BE EXCHANGED FOR A SAILING TICKET
AT PIER OFFICE, LLANDUDNO**

A 3100

Crosville Motor Services Limited

BY ROAD
TO AND FROM
LLANDUDNO
**ISSUED SUBJECT TO THE RESPECTIVE
COMPANIES RULES AND REGULATIONS**

A 3100

Fare | Stage | Date | Serial | Class M/c. No.

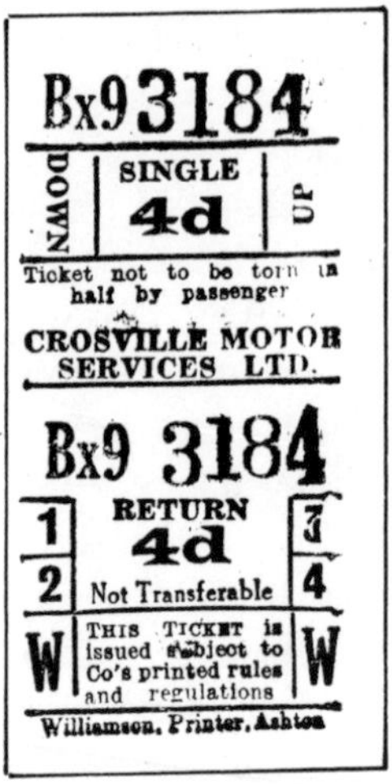

Top right ticket:

Bx9 **3184**

DOWN | **SINGLE 4d** | UP

Ticket not to be torn in
half by passenger

**CROSVILLE MOTOR
SERVICES LTD.**

Bx9 **3184**

1 | **RETURN 4d** | 3
2 | Not Transferable | 4
W | THIS TICKET is
issued subject to
Co's printed rules
and regulations | W

Williamson, Printer, Ashton

Bottom left ticket:

.TD. · CROSVILLE MOTOR SERVICES L'

025 304 738 SINGLE

Issued subject to regulations and conditions published in the Company's
official time tables and notices.

Issued subject to regulatio
ditions published in the
official time tables an

Bottom right ticket:

H22 **1251**

CROSVILLE MOTOR SERVICES LTD. Issued subject to published Rules and Regulations	1d	6/-	EXCHANGE TICKET FOR SERVICE VOUCHER
	2d	7/-	
	3d	8/-	
	4d	9/-	
	5d	10/-	
	6d	11/-	
	1/-	12/-	
	2/-	13/-	
	3/-	14/-	
	4/-	15/-	
	5/-	16/-	

Williamson, Printer, Ashton

Selection of tickets: (*Top left*) Multi-part ticket for insertion into Setright
'speed model' ticket machine. (*Bottom left*) Standard Setright 'speed model'
ticket. (*Top right*) Bell Punch ticket. (*Bottom right*) Exchange ticket for
express service voucher.

company has approximately 2,000 Setright ticket machines in use.

Clerical and inspecting staff numbered 673 in March 1949, but with the introduction of ticket machines this reduced to 637 in 1950 and to 500 in 1953. Further economies made in conjunction with the ticket machines were night safes, originally introduced on a limited basis during World War II which enabled conductors to pay-in their takings without the necessity of a cash-clerk to be on duty. After successful use at Middlewich three were installed at Machynlleth, Dolgellau and Aberaeron, thereby enabling the office to shut at 17.30 and re-open at 09.00. At the big depots Crosville designed and patented a locker system built into a partition known as 'the pigeon loft', which enabled the machine to be placed in the locker which then locked itself so that it could only be withdrawn from the office side of the partition.

Crosville has remained faithful to the Setright system, although limited use has been made in recent years of fareboxes and experiments have taken place with other fare collection equipment as are described in chapters 5 and 6.

Conwy bridge

The Crosville route network in Wales has been affected by two bridges, one across the Menai Straits and the other at Conwy above the main A55 trunk road linking Flint, Denbigh, Cheshire and Lancashire with Caernarfon and Anglesey, crossing the river Conwy by means of a beautiful suspension bridge which was designed by Thomas Telford and opened in 1826. The bridge was single carriageway, protected in later years by traffic lights, and it required a precise knowledge to position a bus at the Conwy end to enter or leave the bridge without catching the side panels. Due to weight restrictions only single-deck buses could use the bridge in passenger service and this necessitated Crosville using more buses than necessary to provide the required seating capacity than would have been needed had double-deck buses been available. The saving was estimated at ten buses, half a million miles and £37,000 per annum at 1951 prices.

In the immediate post-war years Crosville services between Llandudno and Caernarfon, Llandudno and Llanrwst, Llandudno and Conwy via Maesdu or Marl Lane, and Conwy and Old Colwyn used the bridge, together with express services and one or two other local services. Delays to traffic also occurred at the level-crossing (some half-a-mile further along the A55 at Llandudno Junction) where the railway line from Llandudno to Llandudno Junction crossed the road. It was in 1933 that the Ministry of Transport agreed that a new bridge was necessary; by 1951 the old bridge was not only inadequate but dangerous, and even the buses Crosville had been using for many years were classed as too heavy, with the result that passengers had to alight and walk across whilst the bus was driven to the other side. The Caernarfon service was even further hampered by the single-track archway carrying the wall over the main A55 road at the Caernarfon entrance to the town.

On 1 January 1950 a number of Leyland PS1s with MCW bodies (KAs) were placed on the Llandudno – Caernarfon service, together with Bristol L5Gs (KGs) from North Cambrian depots. Owing to the weight restrictions applied to Conwy Bridge and the diversion of the KAs to express service work, the PCs (Beadle bodies with reconditioned 'Cub' running units) replaced them. Seating 35 passengers, these lightweight single-deckers were at first inadequate for the service; the engines were underpowered, and the brakes were weak, so they were improved by the installation of Perkins engines and larger servos. In addition to the PC type there were two Bedfords (SC18 and 19), the C in the classification standing for 'chassisless'. These buses worked several of the Conwy Bridge services until replaced by double-deckers when the new Conwy Bridge was opened in December 1958.

Double-deckers on the North Wales coast

The increased demand for bus services was expressed in dramatic fashion at the North Wales coast depots where Rhyl more than doubled its allocation of buses in comparison with the winter period, and additional buses were allocated to Llandudno town, Llandudno Junction, Llanrwst and Denbigh depots. Additional buses were licenced throughout the Crosville network for the summer, but it was the holiday resorts between Rhyl and Llandudno that attracted the largest number of tourists. In fact, during the early fifties Crosville took nearly 13 percent of their total annual receipts with 19 percent extra vehicles. To achieve this, new vehicles were delivered in spring and vehicles to be replaced kept until after the season, thereby increasing the fleet for the summer peak. Coaches were always made ready out of store, painted and repaired for service by 1 May of each year. Besides the open-top services, double-deckers worked between Denbigh and Llandudno and there were three inter-worked services between Llandudno and Colwyn Bay, Colwyn Bay and Llandudno Junction via Mochdre and Llandudno Junction and Llandudno via Maesdu. The disadvantage of not being able to operate to Conwy is obvious because the single-deckers still had to bear the brunt of the movements to this very popular town, the double-deckers serving as duplicates over the other sections of route. These services were amongst the first to disappear when it was decided to reduce the additional summer commitments.

Seafront services at Rhyl

Crosville first introduced new open-top, double-deck buses for summer use in 1938, but after only two seasons (1938 and 1939) they remained in normal passenger service until the summer of 1952, when these six Leyland TD5s were allocated to Rhyl. In pre-war days they operated in maroon and cream and were allocated to Llandudno depot. The 'toastracks' (described in chapter 7) were worn out and so five second-hand, open-top double-deckers were purchased to meet the requirements for this type of vehicle. In 1950 these were in operation at Rhyl along with the 'toastracks' and six 'E' type petrol-engined single-deckers, nicknamed 'boats' and painted cream. These single-deckers were cut down to the waist-rail, but retained the normal cab with some shelter for the conductor. Wooden slatted seats were provided. They were unique and as far as the public were concerned, a popular vehicle. Limited use was also made of them at Llandudno in competition with the trams. The open-toppers were also used for race meetings and Crosville hired them out for the Grand National, and in later years open-toppers have also been used to convey groups to the Derby.

It is interesting to note that in 1952 Crosville carried out some experiments with radio communication in conjunction with units of the Territorial Army. The results were inconclusive and no further development took place. Operation of the seafront services is very much affected by weather – always a very variable factor in this country.

DUKWS

A fascinating concept was the possibility that a service might be opened across the Dee estuary from Prestatyn to West Kirby using government surplus amphibious vehicles. After trying one of these vehicles in a large pond close to an old brickworks at Warrington, the fact that the DUKW was only capable of 4 knots and had certain other limitations led to the idea being dropped. As a matter of interest, when the road bridge at Bideford was badly damaged by flood water in 1968 the Western National bus service was maintained by army DUKWs, which connected with buses at Appledore and Instow, ferrying passengers across the swollen river.

Opening of Shotton Steel works

An important (and in view of recent circumstances, poignant) event took place on 29 April 1953, when HRH the Duke of Edinburgh visited John Summers Steelworks at Shotton near Chester. Forty coaches were required for two days – all were to be of the latest type, clean, with the paintwork immaculate. The drivers had to have new uniforms, caps with white tops, and be properly rehearsed so that everybody knew what to do. A large number of the vehicles for this hire were assembled at Birkenhead Rock Ferry depot and it was the author's job to supervise their departure, in fleet numerical order, at precise intervals for their initial journey to Shotton. The overall organisation was superb and Crosville was suitably congratulated.

Fares increase 1953

Crosville went for its third fares increase in 1953. Besides all the accountancy work in preparing the necessary financial evidence it was necessary to work out individually from the mileage scale for every fare-table, the new fare and pence per car mile for each fare existing and proposed. I was involved in this exercise and in the North Western area there were 59,268 single fares and 22,739 returns, of which 15,465 singles were increased, 77 reduced and the others remained unaltered. 17,391 returns were increased, nine reduced and the remainder unchanged. In the West Midland and South Wales area there were 5,500 single fares and a corresponding number of returns. After suitable discussion with local authorities, and hearings before the Traffic Commissioners, the revised fares went into operation on 19 April 1953.

Transport Act 1953

Under this Act the machinery for the establishment of area schemes was abolished and the Ministry of Transport was given powers (not exercised within the provisions of this Act) to require the British Transport Commission to relinquish control in the bus companies brought under control of the British Transport Commission, which by 1953 consisted of the Scottish Motor Traction, Thomas Tilling, and Red & White groups.

First post-war bus service economies

Reductions in bus services during the war principally affected the Welsh areas and it is ironic that this situation had the effect of making this area more healthy financially than would have been the case had the mileage been retained. On the other hand, the services in the English areas were overloaded, but the additional revenue served to cross-subsidise the unremunerative services in Wales, which by 1939 were being supported by the English portion. The local authorities could not, or would not, understand this situation and demanded full restitution of pre-war services. One such service not re-introduced after World War II was that between Rhos-on-Sea (Abbey Road) and Colwyn Bay (Station), which had a particularly interesting history. Commenced about 1929 by the North Wales Silver, this originally operated from Abbey Road via Colwyn Bay Station to Old Colwyn (Tan Lan) and was in competition with the Llandudno trams as it operated parallel to their route in Rhos-on-Sea, then common with it to Alexandra Road (Colwyn Bay), but thence direct to Colwyn Bay Station, rejoining part of the tram route to Old Colwyn. As the bus route served the newly-developed areas it abstracted traffic from the trams. Eventually the Colwyn Bay – Old Colwyn section was linked to the Colwyn Bay – Conwy service and the only journeys retained on the Abbey Road service until discontinued in 1939 were those which connected at Colwyn Bay Station with the outward and return journeys of the Llandudno – Manchester 'club train'.

Discussions took place and some mileage was restored and other improved facilities were provided by linking services to provide a greater choice of destinations. Arising from increased costs the winter of 1951/52 showed that whilst a reasonable loss would have to be maintained in the Welsh area, there was a danger that it would swamp the company. Fares were increased and at the same time a decision was taken to reduce mileage. Although the extensive negotiations with local authorities took up most of the winter of 1952/53 the resultant effect was a significant reduction in mileage, which at the time was sufficient to meet the company's immediate requirements.

Abandonment of the Llandudno trams

Many and hard had been the battles fought out between Crosville and the Llandudno trams. At management level, one side or another had protested to the other over time or alleged infringements of agreements. Buses had obstructed trams at stops, and racing had taken place on the section between Penrhynside and Craig-y-don to see who could pick up the traffic at Carmen Sylva Road and Queens Road stops. Indeed, on occasion, blows had been exchanged between employees of the rival undertakings and as early as 21 September 1930 Crosville buses replaced the trams on the section of tramway which was then abandoned between Colwyn Bay (Greenfield Road) and Old Colwyn (Queens Hotel). During 1953 and 1954 the Llandudno and Colwyn Electric Railway Co Ltd made a financial loss. Passenger loadings were declining – if the trams were to continue running it would be necessary to spend a lot of money in repairs and renewals. The Board of Directors, therefore, announced that the trams would be replaced with buses, and this occurred on 25 March 1956, the last tram operating on the previous day. Competition between the now competing bus undertakings involved the tramway company's buses serving Colwyn Bay station, but following a common route between Penrhynside and Llandudno (West Shore) except that the tramway company buses diverted via Nant-y-gamar Road to Mostyn Avenue to rejoin the original route of the tramway.

Conversion to buses was not the answer to the financial problems of the company given the trend of costs, revenue and passengers prevalent in the road passenger transport industry, and in 1961 the directors of the L&CBE Railway Co Ltd had accepted the offer of £40,000 for the goodwill of the business. No assets of the company were purchased, although several members of the staff were taken into Crosville employment. As a result of the purchase Crosville took the opportunity of re-organising its routes in the area and with the approval of the Traffic Commissioners, the revised bus services came into operation on 28 May 1961.

Post Offices buses

The passenger-carrying mail-bus operated by the Post Office at Llanidloes commenced on 20 February 1957 and further services of this kind have since been introduced in Crosville's operating area.

Renumbering of bus services

With the introduction of the summer timetable on 5 July 1959 Crosville brought into operation a completely new method of service numbering whereby areas received prefix letters followed by numbers from 1 upwards. The new arrangements provided for the following grouping: Flint and Holywell A1–55, Mold B1–41, Chester area C1–91, Wrexham and Oswestry D1–96 also originally 'E' and G1–63, Wirral area F1–90, Liverpool and Warrington H1–41, Runcorn area J1–55, Crewe and Nantwich K1–75, Llandudno, Rhyl and Denbigh M1–99 and P1–4, Holyhead, Bangor and Caernarfon N1–99, Pwllheli and Ffestiniog R1–39, Aberystwyth and Barmouth S1–38 and express services X1–70.

The combination of letters and numerals gave 832 combinations instead of the previous 373, but when one considers that 24 services in Crewe which were all grouped under 207 became K1–24 the reason becomes apparent. The old numbers 1–58 went into the A,B,C group; 101–76 into F,H,J; 201–25 into K; 301–64 into D,E,G; 401–60 into M,P; 501–74 into N,R; and 601–39 into S.

With acquisition of the former North Western services in 1972 the letter 'E' was used for services in the Northwich, Macclesfield and Congleton areas and the Wrexham local services were renumbered. Bus services on the Runcorn 'busway' received the prefix letter 'T'. As services have changed in the last twenty years new numbers appeared and others have disappeared with the withdrawal of other services. Limited stop services, including the *Cymru Coastliner* are prefixed 'L'.

5

Retrenchment in the sixties

New Conwy Bridge

On 13 December 1958 the new bridge was opened to traffic and the next day revised Crosville bus services came into operation. In general terms this meant the substitution of double-deckers for single-deckers, with consequent economies and associated timetable changes. The old archway was made one way and a new road built around the town walls, entering through another arch, with the result that there is a gyratory traffic scheme in operation. The new flyover across the railway line level-crossing at Llandudno Junction removed another traffic bottleneck so matters were considerably eased.

Widnes – Runcorn Bridge

The opening of another bridge on 21 July 1961, this time in the northern part of the company's operating area, enabled other significant improvements to bus services to be made. The new Widnes – Runcorn Bridge replaced the old car transporter service and for the first time Crosville was able to offer through bus services from Chester and Runcorn to Widnes and Liverpool.

Transport Act 1962

This Act placed the shareholdings of the government-owned bus undertakings, including Crosville, under the newly-formed Transport Holding Company.

Cymru Coastliner

Apart, perhaps, from the *Trawscambria* this is one of the company's most interesting routes and provides an hourly 'limited stop' service between Chester, Flint, Rhyl and Llandudno, with certain journeys being extended via Bangor to Caernarfon. It was introduced on 5 September 1965 as part of a major revision of bus services along the North Wales coast and at the same time, the Chester – Rhyl, Rhyl – Llandudno, and Llandudno – Caernarfon stage services were linked to provide a half-hourly through stage carriage service from Chester to Caernarfon.

Due to operational problems it was decided to split the stage service at Rhyl with separate but connecting Chester – Rhyl and Rhyl – Caernarfon services, while in more recent years the Rhyl – Caernarfon service has been again divided into Rhyl – Llandudno and Llandudno – Caernarfon services, so reverting to the arrangement which applied prior to the introduction of the revisions in 1965.

Promenade services

These have been a feature of the summer bus services at Rhyl for many years and they have operated spasmodically in the Llandudno area. However, the number in use was progressively halved, and about 1960 an open-top service operated from Prestatyn to Abergele (Gwrych Castle), but this was reduced to run between Winkups Camp and Robin Hood camp. In more recent years open-top services have been developed and are now back to Prestatyn (serving the new Pontins) as a service through to Abergele (Pensarn Station).

Runcorn New Town

During 1966 the master plan for Runcorn New Town was confirmed and Crosville, as the principal bus operator in the area, accepted the opportunity to co-operate with Runcorn

Development Corporation in developing a new concept in public transport – a buses-only track – and for the first time a whole town of some 100,000 persons was planned and designed around the public transport system.

Service reductions

The developments described above – in particular the imaginative concept of the Cymru Coastliner – were matched in September 1966 by the largest single set of service withdrawals since the end of World War II. The area most affected by the service cuts was the Vale of Clwyd (involving Denbigh depot), together with a smaller number of withdrawals in the Pwllheli area. The full list is as follows:-

Services withdrawn 19 September 1966
M44   Abergele–Glascoed
M52   Denbigh–Wern–Tyn Celyn
M53   Ruthin–Graigadwywynt
M55   Denbigh–Llanynys–Ruthin
M58   Denbigh–Deunant
M63   Denbigh–Peniel
M64   Denbigh–Llannefydd–Abergele
M66   Denbigh–Bwlch
M71   Ruthin–Clocaenog–Old Toll Bar
M73   Ruthin–Cyffylliog
M74   Ruthin–Rhewl Smithy
M77   Ruthin–Hirwaen–Denbigh
R8   Llangwynadl–Aberdaron
R12   Pwllheli–Garn Fadryn–Uwchmynydd
R13/5 Pwllheli–Brynmawr
R17/8 Sarn Bach–Ysgubor Hen

Services withdrawn 4 December 1966
D74   Oswestry–Crewe Green
D75   Oswestry/Burgedin–Welshpool
D78   Oswestry–Gronwen Circular

In addition numerous journeys were withdrawn from services in the Wrexham area with a consequent reduction in mileage, but without cessation of services. At about the same time, revisions to services, particularly in the Crewe and Chester areas, brought about a similar situation, although beside mileage reductions some bus services were also withdrawn.

National Bus Company

Further moves in the changing pattern of bus ownership came about in 1968 and 1969. During 1968 there was much discussion both inside and outside Parliament of the controversial clauses of the government's new Transport Bill. In the midst of all this it was announced that BET had agreed to sell its bus interests in Great Britain to the Transport Holding Company. An enabling Act was passed, authorising the Transport Holding Company to increase its borrowing powers to carry out this major purchase. The Transport Bill finally became the Transport Act 1968, which among other things replaced the Transport Holding Company with the National Bus Company (NBC) from 1 January 1969. The Transport Act changed the regulations relating to drivers' hours, and gave powers to local authorities to make grants towards the maintenance of unremunerative bus services. Both were matters which were to have a significant effect on bus operators in the nineteen seventies.

The National Bus Company was conceived as a means of offering the public and local authorities a progressive, dependable bus system. The structure of the company gives bus systems local control supported by central policy-making. As an organisation it currently employs around 58,000 people and owns approximately 15,600 buses and coaches. The NBC is a holding company with some 40 subsidiary companies and groups – each subsidiary is required by statute to be separately accountable as far as finances are concerned.

To ensure that continuing consultation and co-operation between British Rail and NBC subsidiaries exists, the standing joint committees of responsible officials established in the early

Above: MB255, one of the first post-war ECW bodied Bristols at Liverpool (Pier Head). Note the livery and full destination indicator display. (*Crosville*)

Below: KA1, a pre-war Leyland TS7 with post-war Saro body at Rhyl alongside a Bristol K type double deck. The indicator on the KA has been changed from the original flap type. (*C. Shears*)

Above: MG630 at Rhyl. This Bristol G05G was purchased secondhand from the Brighton Company in 1951. (*C. Shears*)

Below: GA15, a Leyland LT5A dating from 1934 (G15) with replacement post second world war Leyland 8.6 litre engine and Burlington body. (*C. Shears*)

years of railway involvement with bus operation, continues to meet at frequent intervals to discuss and agree matters of common concern.

One of the obvious outward signs has been the corporate identity of the vehicles, buildings and staff uniforms featuring the double 'N' symbol. Buses are now in common liveries of green or red, with coaches in white livery.

The Transport Act 1968 enabled the Ministry of Transport to make grants towards the capital cost of new buses, provided they conformed to certain standard specifications, which placed emphasis on vehicles (both single- and double-deck) for one-man operation. One-man operation is no new thing, dating back to the earliest days of bus transport, as will be seen from references in previous chapters of this book, but the wide-scale introduction of single-manning on intensive city services, using double-deckers with sophisticated electronic ticket-issuing machines, is a new development; it is this aspect of general economy that the provisions of the Act are designed to promote. An important aspect of one-man operation is the easement of staff shortages; it also gives greater job satisfaction to the employee which has many beneficial results, not the least being a reduction in staff turnover. Labour costs represent more than 70 percent of the operators' outgoings and anything which can help to keep this figure down, by increasing the productivity of bus crews, is bound to result in a better service to the travelling public; if costs rise too high, fares have to be increased and in some cases services have to be drastically reduced or abandoned.

Under the organisation of the National Bus Co Crosville formed part of the North Western region along with Cumberland, North Western, Ribble and Standerwick.

Investiture of HRH the Prince of Wales

Crosville took a leading part in the transport arrangements for the investiture of HRH the Prince of Wales in Caernarfon Castle in 1969, the company's general manager being a member of the transport committee for the investiture. Special services provided included shuttle services between special car parks and Caernarfon, and the conveyance of all important guests from the railway station to the Castle. In addition to the company's own vehicles, fifty double-deck buses were hired for the occasion from other NBC subsidiaries, municipal and independent operators, together with their drivers, who had to be billeted in temporary accommodation in a local school.

Fare boxes

The sixties featured many developments in fare collection and Crosville carried out a number of experiments with fare boxes, a means by which the passenger deposits the fare for the journey being undertaken into a sealed container, under the control and in the view of the driver. First introduced at Chester in March 1969 on local service C40 to Upton, they were in due course used on other local services in Chester, at Heswall on the local services and F19 to Birkenhead (Woodside), at Wrexham on the Queens Park Services, on Crewe town services, on Runcorn 'busway' services, Rhyl local and circular services, Aberystwyth – Penparcau, and at Liverpool on H12 to Prescot.

At first Johnson boxes were used, then some Bande-Keene models and later Setrights, but due to difficulty in obtaining the correct fares, withdrawals and replacements with standard Setright ticket-issuing machines commenced at Runcorn in 1975 and was completed with Heswall in 1977.

Acquired operators

During August 1969 the business of Meredith & Jesson of Cefn Mawr was acquired, while J. W. Lloyd of Oswestry was taken-over in 1961 and brought Crosville an Oswestry local service.

Rail replacement bus services

The era of closures of railway branch lines and little-used railway stations on retained lines, arising from the Beeching

Report of 1963, involved Crosville in the provision of a number of alternative bus services.

Where substitute bus services have been provided to meet rail closures they have in general proved to be completely unremunerative. This did not matter so much while the railways were liable for the payment of a subsidy to the bus companies to cover its losses for the provision of the replacement bus services, but the Transport Act 1968 freed the railways of this obligation and left the burden squarely in the lap of the National Bus Company through its subsidiaries. The companies therefore took the only course open to them and wherever possible withdrew from the operations of these highly unremunerative rail replacement services.

6

The Seventies

1970 – A disastrous year

'The year 1970 was a disastrous one for the bus industry and the National Bus Company was affected in much the same way as were other operators', so began the National Bus Company's annual report for 1970. Not only was there a more rapid rate of inflation and prices, but the reduced driving time permitted by the revised drivers' hours regulations brought about a loss of flexibility and a consequent loss of earnings by drivers, which added to the problems of recruiting and retaining staff. The problem was therefore to determine in 1971 how bus services – even those carrying a substantial number of passengers – could be retained, and who would pay for them.

Against this background should be considered the political situation, insofar as the powers granted to local authorities under the Transport Act 1968 had perhaps not really been appreciated by the elected representatives and officers of the authorities concerned, whereas escalating costs and reducing traffic had led Crosville to carry out an extensive review of all its stage carriage services. The outcome of the review was an official announcement by Crosville in December 1970 to the eleven county councils in its operating area, which informed them that some 200 loss-making stage carriage services could well cease after 13 March 1971 if financial assistance was not forthcoming, and that beside removing buses from rural areas several towns and villages could also lose their bus services.

Not only would the public have suffered but some 700

Crosville staff would have been made redundant, with the closure of depots at Aberystwyth, Aberaeron, Llanidloes, Machynlleth, Dolgellau, Pwllheli, Blaenau Ffestiniog and Llangefni/Amlwch and the reduction in the fleet by 275 buses.

The reaction was predictable, with Crosville being accused of blackmail in only giving three months' notice of possible abandonment of routes, and the issue was the subject of a question in Parliament. It was further suggested that the company should cross-subsidise its services, which demonstrated a clear lack of understanding of the company's position insofar as this had been the practice of bus company finance for some forty years or more. Indeed the urban and inter-urban riders had paid fares at a level which enabled their rural counterparts to enjoy bus services operated on an unremunerative basis but at a comparable level of fares.

Happily the situation was resolved and good sense prevailed, with the result that most of the facilities were preserved. However, the situation could not be left and substantial service revisions took place, particularly in Mid-Wales where the Crosville and former BET subsidiary Western Welsh, met at Aberystwyth, an arrangement which lasted until April 1972 when Crosville began to take over the Western Welsh operation, the final phase taking place in December 1972. The substantial cost savings achieved in 1971 by elimination of many rural operations, resulted in a profit being made in that year which was followed in 1972 by a further improvement in the financial position.

Mid Wales Motorways Ltd

A particularly interesting event had occurred on 15 February 1970 when Crosville took over the Mid Wales Motorways Ltd services between Four Crosses and Shrewsbury (D74) and Shrewsbury – Welshpool – Newton (D75). No vehicles were involved but it is worth noting that the Crosville depot at Llandrindod Wells and the associated bus services had been transferred to Mid Wales Motorways Ltd. in the nineteen fifties.

Transport Act 1972

Another major development affecting public transport was the passing of the Local Government Act of 1972, which came into operation on 1 April 1974 in England and Wales and 1 April 1975 in Scotland. Among its many wide-reaching provisions, which reorganised the entire set-up of local authorities, this Act placed a much wider responsibility for transport on County Councils and Metropolitan Counties. They became responsible for the co-ordination of all forms of public passenger transport within their areas and were enjoined to submit 'Transportation Policies and Programmes' annually to the Secretary of State for the Environment.

At last the way seemed open for the overall control and co-ordination of transport and traffic, including traffic management schemes in city centres for placing the emphasis on public rather than private transport. County engineers or county surveyors set up departments within their organisations presided over by a transport manager (or equivalent title) to discharge the counties' obligations under the Act. The Act left the running of municipally-owned bus fleets with the second-tier authorities (the district or city councils) and did not transfer them to the county councils, which became co-ordinators and policy-makers rather than actual operators. These provisions entailed the spending of a great deal of public money in the establishment of transport and traffic patterns directed towards the well-being of the community at large. The situation may be summarised by quoting part of Section 203 of the Local Government Act 1972, which gives county councils the duty 'to provide a co-ordinated and efficient system of passenger transport'.

Management changes

In 1972 the National Bus Co. management structure was re-organised into three regions and Crosville went into the Western region (along with Cumberland, Ribble, PMT, Midland Red,

Western Welsh, Red & White, Jones Omnibus, South Wales Transport and Oxford South Midland).

Crosville in Cardiganshire

Aberystwyth is the largest town in Central Wales, being both a seaside resort and a university town with a resident population of 12,000 persons. Crosville has been in Aberystwyth since 1924 when it established competing services with the bus services provided by the Great Western Railway. With the acquisition of Wrexham Transport and several local independants Crosville became the principal bus operator in the area. In fact the early role of buses in Cardiganshire was as rail feeders, and all bus routes entering Aberystwyth had as their terminus a site adjoining the railway station. An area agreement was reached with Western Welsh which had established depots at New Quay (Cardiganshire) and Newcastle Emlyn (Carmarthenshire). Western Welsh entered Aberystwyth on its service from Ammanford with buses outstationed at Lampeter and Crosville passed through New Quay on the service between Aberystwyth and Cardigan.

Crosville introduced town services into Aberystwyth in 1948 and operated a seasonal service along the sea front, using the last of the fleet of Shelvoke and Drewery toastracks. One-man operation of routes in the area commenced in 1963 and 1970 saw complete conversion.

The local authority policy which evolved set out to preserve as far as possible the route network but to reduce frequencies and delete unnecessary journeys, and it is particularly interesting to see how the new Act worked in the context of a very rural part of Wales. It should be appreciated that outside Aberystwyth the area is one of sparse population and the main peak-hour movements are made by schoolchildren.

Aberystwyth depot is the location of the area superintendent and there is a depot at Aberaeron and numerous outstations.

The small depot at Machynlleth operates a few workings on S13 and S14 into Aberystwyth, but Crosville's first route from the town along the A44 was eastwards to Ponterwyd, with a seasonal extension south to Devils Bridge. Further along the A44, Llanidloes is connected to Aberystwyth by a Mondays-only service. Many years earlier the GWR had run a spectacular seasonal service from the narrow-gauge station at Devil's Bridge to the summit of Plynlimon using a half-tracked Morris Commercial. Another operator who provides a service into Aberystwyth from the east is D. J. Evans of Penrhyncoch, who purchased the business of Morgan of Penrhyncoch in 1959. Lloyd Jones of Pontrhydygroes ran a stage service on Mondays and Saturdays from Yspytty Ystwyth via Pontrhydygroes and Llanfhanyel-y-Creddyr to Aberystwyth but ceased its operation in 1970. However, in December 1971, Crosville resumed the stage route on Mondays (S19), but working it from the Aberystwyth end and avoiding some of the more torturous lanes used by Jones' service.

The sparseness of the population in the hinterland behind Aberystwyth is where some of the county's worst loss-making services operate, including the S9 Aberystwyth – Pontrhydfendigaid – Tregaron which meets up there with services operated to that town from Llangeithio, Lampeter and Pontrhydfendigaid by David Jones of Llangeithio, who had succeeded T. Jones (Perris Motors) who had run a stage service from Aberaeron to Tregaron until the late 1950s. South Cardiganshire is perhaps more sparsely populated but bus services were introduced by both Western Welsh and independants; all these were severely reduced in the late fifties and sixties, leaving little for Crosville to take-over on 23 April 1972 when the company absorbed the Western Welsh depots at Newcastle Emlyn and New Quay. On the same date the South Wales Transport Lampeter operations (three staff and two vehicles) together with the Aberystwyth –Ammanford service became part of Crosville. Crosville continues to operate from Newcastle Emlyn to Llangrannog and Aberporth, to which place Richards of Moylegrove provides a service from Cardigan.

All routes entering Aberystwyth from the south approach the town on the A487 from Penparcau, where there is a substantial housing estate that is served relatively frequently for much of the day. In the early 1970s Bristol RELL6G buses equipped with fare boxes, replaced the *Lodekka* vehicles which had hitherto operated on this service, but the fare boxes were soon withdrawn.

By 1973 Cardiganshire County Council, which met all revenue support applications for two years, had come to the conclusion that in September of that year there should be some pruning of services; as a result the Aberystwyth – Devil's Bridge service S8 extension to Cwmystwyth, Saturday diversion on S9 to Brynafan and the former Western Welsh services out of Newcastle Emlyn would cease operation. It was not long afterwards that the public transport responsibilities of Cardiganshire County Council ceased, for in April 1974, as part of the re-organisation of local government, Dyfed County Council was formed with Cardiganshire as a district named Ceredigion, within the new county. The new county council developed the transport policies established by Cardiganshire and set out in its 1975 (first) Transport Policies and Programmes document its main objectives for public transport in Dyfed, which are that the public transport network should be more closely co-ordinated and that there should be equitable balance of costs and benefits both geographically and socially.

The situation whereby there are heavy peak movements of schoolchildren has given the county council an opportunity to develop off-peak facilities at marginal costs and as a result Ceredigion has seen an increase in off-peak market day facilities since 1974. As many independent operators use part-time labour to cover school contracts it has meant that Crosville has probably been more involved, but there are exceptions. Interestingly the policy of Cardiganshire County Council was reviewed when, in April 1977, S8 was reinstated to Cwmystwyth and Llanfihangel-y-Creuddyn was served on Monday, seven years after Lloyd Jones withdrew from the route in June 1970. Crosville's partial replacement service (S19) was extended in April 1977 to Ffair Rhos. These additional facilities were further improved some nine months later when S19 and S9 were linked as a circular, resuming regular weekday running to rural areas which lost their bus services in 1965. Further other limited facilities have been provided in the Aberaeron area by means of Section 30 permits (an arrangement whereby fare-paying passengers may be carried on school contracts). David Jones of Llangeitho commenced new off-peak services in July 1975 on varying days of the week from Cilian Aeron to Lampeter, Cribyn to Aberaeron and Cellan to Aberystwyth.

Arising from discussions between the company and the Gwynedd and Dyfed County Councils, the spring of 1976 saw a number of revisions to services. A through Aberystwyth – Machynlleth – Dolgellau service (in replacement of shorter services) commenced with onward connections at Dolgellau to Wrexham and Caernarfon, the Aberystwyth – Cardigan service connects with Richards of Moylegrove's Cardigan – Fishguard – Haverfordwest service, through fares being available. It can be fairly commented that bus services in the area have improved since the fifties and sixties and as public passenger transport arrangements are not static it is interesting to observe the further developments described in chapter 7, which have occurred as a result of the Crosville Market Analysis Project surveys in Ceredigion in 1978.

Concessionary fares

Crosville's first concessionary fares scheme for old age pensioners came into operation at Holyhead in June 1970, at Crewe in July 1970, and at Whiston in August of that year. These set the pattern for numerous 'token' and 'pass' concessionary fare arrangements which have been introduced throughout Crosville's operating area.

Transfer of North Western

On 25 November 1971 it was announced that the South East Lancashire and North East Cheshire Passenger Transport Executive was negotiating to acquire the stage carriage bus services of the North Western Road Car Co Ltd operated within the SELNEC designated area. Discussion had been taking place since early 1970 and the actual transfer took place on 1 January 1972. As part of the new arrangements Crosville acquired the North Western depots at Macclesfield and Northwich (where Crosville had attempted to commence bus services some sixty years previously) together with a large number of buses and staff and most western operations from Biddulph, where the depot was owned by PMT. In addition Crosville took over the Warrington – Altrincham/Urmston group of services previously operated from North Western's Altringham depot, which went to SELNEC. There were no buses for this and as a result Crosville acquired five Leyland Leopards from Yorkshire Woollen. The buses at the North Western Warrington outstation also came under Crosville control and by arrangement with SELNEC, Crosville buses commenced operating into Manchester from the newly-acquired Macclesfield depot which worked the service. The North Western coaches were not part of the transfer to either SELNEC or Crosville and were eventually to form, with Standerwick, the basis of the newly-formed National Travel (North West) Ltd. During 1974 there was a comprehensive programme of service revisions in the Greater Manchester area, and on 27 April in the same year Crosville took-over a number of Lancashire United Transport (LUT) bus services in the Warrington area. No vehicles were involved in the transfer. During 1972 the whole of the issued share capital of LUT Ltd was acquired by a company named Lanaten Ltd. The offer to the shareholders of LUT by Lanaten was made in concert with SELNEC in that the Executive guaranteed the funds required to purchase the shares. Various clauses were included in a new agreement signed on 8 December 1972 between the SELNEC Executive, Lanaten and LUT, which amongst other matters gave the Executive an option to acquire the shares of LUT on or after 1 January 1976 at the same cost as was incurred by Lanaten. In July 1980 it was announced that LUT was to be merged with the rest of Greater Manchester Transport and lose the LUT fleet name from 31 March 1981.

That section of the North Western Road Car Co Ltd which

operated stage carriage services within the designated area was acquired by SELNEC on 3 March 1972. The company which had been formed to carry out these bus services was re-named SELNEC Cheshire Bus Co Ltd and was a wholly-owned subsidiary of the executive. In 1973 the operations of this company were rationalised and integrated into the Executive's divisional structure. The remaining garages, vehicles and personnel of North Western in Derbyshire were transferred to the Trent Motor Traction Co Ltd.

Cheshire

As a contrast to West Wales it is useful to consider the local authority's position in Cheshire, Crosville's home county, where the company is the largest stage carriage operator. This county supported rural bus services under section 34 of the Transport Act 1968 when the company gave its notice of substantial service withdrawals. The county then established a working party to study any problems arising from withdrawals of bus services but with the basic policy of retaining the services until the position had been carefully examined.

Since 1 April 1974 all Cheshire's transportation activities have come under one control, and now there is a Strategic Planning Transportation Committee which has three sub-committees covering public transport, planning and highways. A transport board, consisting of chief officers of the county council, takes a corporate view and makes recommendations. Within the Department of Highways and Transportation there is a transport unit whose director is responsible to the transport board in regard to public transport and transport policy. During 1976 major service revisions were undertaken in the Newcastle-under-Lyme and Crewe areas flanking the Cheshire/Staffordshire border.

Cheshire's Public Transport Plan

Cheshire County Council's 1979 Public Transport Plan set out to achieve county-wide savings of £400,000 by operational efficiency together with a slight reduction in the average level of service throughout Cheshire, in order to reduce the operating deficits of operators. Accordingly, detailed area surveys were carried out in 1978 and where appropriate, further information derived from Crosville's own Market Analysis Project surveys, has been analysed in conjunction with the county council surveys. As a result reports were published in December 1979 in regard to bus services in the Ellesmere Port and Neston area and in the Congleton area, the outcome of which is described later in this history.

Ellesmere Port

Sixteen vehicles are based at Ellesmere Port where there is office accommodation at the bus station, but as there are no garage facilities only sweeping-out and minor mechanical repairs are undertaken, buses being refuelled and maintained at Chester depot.

Runcorn 'Busway'

It was announced in February 1971 that Runcorn New Town's public transport system was to be called 'Busway' and the first seven miles were formally opened on 29 October 1971 by Eldon Griffiths, MP, Parliamentary Under-Secretary of the Department of the Environment, by unveiling a plaque at Castlefields. Active 'Busway' services had been operating since 14 October 1971 and a general revision of bus services in the Runcorn area took place on 31 October. The 'Busway' provides a rapid-transit system for single-deck buses, running on a reserved track originally with fare collection by means of fare boxes. At Runcorn a close relationship to the ideal linear form has been attained whereby the ideal has been modified into a chain of new residential areas forming a figure of eight with the town centre at its intersection and the new industrial areas linked to the chain by spurs and loops. Communities, each having a population of about 8,000 have been planned along the track like beads on a

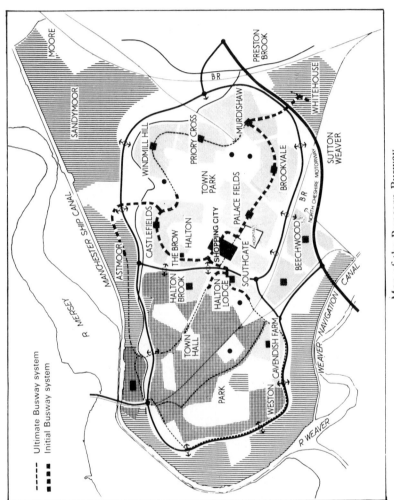

Map of the Runcorn Busway.

string, and no one will reside more than 500yd or five minutes' walking distance from a bus stop. Close liason was maintained by Crosville and the development corporation throughout the period of development of the proposals.

There is a new central bus station at Shopping City, opened on 4 November 1972, for non-'Busway' services. There is a direct link including escalators between the bus station on the 'Busway' and that for other buses. As part of the general service revisions the Chester, Frodsham, Runcorn service was extended to serve Shopping City, while Widnes Corporation and Crosville introduced two new joint services from Whiston and from Bold Heath or Farnworth via Widnes.

Runcorn Busway logo.

An interesting feature of the 'Busway' design is that the scales have been deliberately weighted in the buses' favour insofar as it is generally more convenient to use the bus rather than a car. The 22ft wide roads are designed for a maximum speed of 40mph with the services attaining an average of 21–22mph, and it was the first major project to rank for an infrastructure grant from the then Ministry of Transport under the terms of the 1968 Transport Act. This amounted to a 75 percent grant towards constructional costs. By 1975 the 'Busway' services came near to breaking even on the revenue account. On 22 May 1977 the final sections of the 'Busway' were opened, bringing the total length to 11.37 miles. The completion of the 'Busway' was accompanied by the introduction of a revised network of bus services designed jointly by Crosville and Cheshire County Council, one of the features being the integration of services on the 'Busway' with longer established town services in Old Runcorn. From 22 May all town services operated to and from the high-level bus station at Shopping City, whereas the other services operated from the low-level bus station. Further developments in Runcorn were the trial operation on the 'Busway' in November 1978 of a Volvo articulated bus, to assess the scope for this type of vehicle, and the introduction on 2 December 1979 of a new limited-stop service between Runcorn and North Wales. Called the 'Town-Lynx', it runs between Runcorn, Ellesmere Port, Queensferry, Buckley, Flint and Mold. The service is operated by Leyland Leopards with Duple Dominant II bodies, which are painted in green with light green lower panels and featuring a striking design of a big black cat leaping along the side of the bus. This distinctive symbol is emphasised by the words 'TOWN LYNX'.

Merseyside

The Transport Act 1968 empowered the Minister of Transport to set up passenger transport authorities and executives as thought fit. In 1969 four such bodies were created, two of which affected Crosville, namely the PTEs at Merseyside (MPTE) and Greater Manchester (SELNEC). The authority is a body consisting of elected representatives and is responsible for overall policy and financial control. The executive is made up of full-time professional officers and is responsible for the day-to-day operation of the transport undertaking. The Merseyside Passenger Transport Authority was therefore established on 1 April 1969. The executive took up office in November of that year, with formal vesting of the assets of the former Liverpool, Birkenhead and Wallasey municipal undertakings in the PTE taking place on 1 December 1969, when the PTE assumed responsibility for 1,300 buses and seven vessels.

Among the various duties placed on the PTE by the 1968 Transport Act, is one that requires the PTE to take into account services provided by British Rail and the National Bus Co and

Above: M170, a pre-war Leyland with replacement oil engine, and refurbished body at Colwyn Bay in the 1950s. (*C. Shears*)

Below: U13, a Shelvroke and Drury toast rack in post Second World War livery at Aberystwyth. Standing, second from left, is the late Captain E. Roberts, Traffic Manager of Crosville. (*Crosville*)

Above: Line-up of coaches: from left to right, KW241 (ECW/Bristol LL6B), SL55 (Duple/Bedford OB), KA177 (Harrington/Leyland Tiger TS8) and LFM317 (MCW/Leyland PS1). (*Crosville*)
Below: E61, Leyland LT3 used for sea-front services. (*C. Shears*)

this, of course, meant Crosville (and Ribble, which company is not part of this history) which had over the years evolved agreements with the three municipalities concerned. These agreements involved restrictions and protective fares which were in conflict with the PTE's duty 'to secure or promote the provision of a properly integrated and efficient system of public passenger transport to meet the needs of the area'. As a result of extensive discussions and negotiations between the MPTE and Crosville an agreement dated 30 January 1972 replaced all the previous arrangements and placed the Crosville services in the stipulated area, both in respect of timetables and fares, under the control of the PTE, which guarantees Crosville a financial return on all area mileage calculated on the base year of 1969. The new situation gave the PTE the opportunity to examine the overall requirements for the area and adjust the facilities as necessary in the best interests of all concerned. The Local Government Act of 1972, however, made Merseyside a metropolitan county and increased the geographical area of responsibility of the MPTE by including from 1974 the municipal bus fleets of Southport and St Helens, together with further NBC mileage within the area of jurisdiction.

On the date the new agreement came into effect (30 January 1972), Crosville buses commenced picking-up and setting-down passengers without restriction within the area of the MPTE, and charged MPTE fares. There was no change on Crosville services between Bromborough and Woodside or on services F17, F18 and F24 because of operational difficulties. The new arrangement did, however, apply to all 'H' routes out of Liverpool, but as Crosville buses do not stop at all the MPTE stops notices are displayed on the affected bus stops indicating the nearest pick-up point. At the same time services H1 and H25 were re-routed in the Catherine Street area of Liverpool to follow the MPTE route past the Women's Hospital and the Philharmonic Hall instead of turning down Canning Street and Upper Duke Street.

In Merseyside new interchange facilities have been installed by the County Council at two suburban stations on the upgraded local rail system, for the benefit of passengers using NBC services operated by agreement. Discussions were still in hand regarding a new agreement between the PTE and the NBC subsidiaries to follow upon an original agreement which was due to expire at the end of 1978.

On Sunday, 1 April 1979, the MPTE introduced the largest re-organisation of bus services ever introduced in the Wirral. Crosville, with its depots at Rock Ferry, Heswall and West Kirby, had operated services throughout the area since the 1920s and in general terms provided facilities from Heswall to Birkenhead, West Kirby to Birkenhead, New Ferry to Heswall, local and linking services in the non-municipal area, with services to other parts of Cheshire and North Wales. The municipalities at Birkenhead and Wallasey had their own local groups of services besides inter-running between the two towns. Crosville was involved with both municipalities and as part of the 1930 agreement Birkenhead Corporation ran through to Heswall. Since the establishment of the PTE in 1972 service revisions in the Wirral had been comparatively few, but the 1979 changes in general provided for some rationalisation with a saving of 25 PTE buses, frequency reductions on most services not affected by route rationalisation, while maintaining the proportion of mileage operated by Crosville, general abandonment of National Bus Co areas, an observance of all bus stops on services worked by Crosville, and in some areas an exchange of operators.

Crosville came off the routes linking West Kirby, Moreton and Birkenhead (Park Station) or Wallasey, but new services linking Birkenhead (Woodside) and West Kirby and operating via Park Station were operated in their place. Opportunity was taken to incorporate the F27 from Woodside to Caldy, West Kirby and Meols and the 79/80 Prenton Circular into the new group of services, now numbered 80 – 82. Concurrent with the service revisions a scheme of standardised route numbering came into effect with Crosville allocated numbers in the 72 – 89 range (with the exception of 80B which is used by MPTE buses for a supplementary service between Woodside and Arrowe Park).

Services C22/C23 between Chester and Meols were truncated at West Kirby and improvements were made to F40/F41 (New Ferry – Heswall) which were extended on to West Kirby and numbered 83/84. A new service 85 linking Eastham Ferry and West Kirby and operating via Mill Park Estate, Bromborough, Thornton Hough, Heswall, Irby, Greasby and Newton completed the revised network in the area. Services F9 – F11 between Birkenhead and North Wales were re-routed via Eastham Village Road and F15 (renumbered 89) Wood-side–Burton, now proceeds via Old Chester Road, Lower Bebington, Spital, Plymyard Avenue and Mill Park. The outcome has been that apart from certain works' services the inner section of New Chester Road is served exclusively by Crosville buses.

Heswall local services F25 – 26 were renumbered 78/79 and the extensive route network between Heswall and Woodside (F19 – F24) provided by Crosville was renumbered 72–77. A new diversion (72A) was introduced via Fishers Lane to replace the PTE-operated service 471 between Irby and Woodside. Services F17/F18 between Woodside and Parkgate received numbers 87/88 with a re-routing in Church Road instead of Borough Road, and now provides a direct link between St Catherines and Clatterbridge Hospital. Not unnaturally, the extensive changes took several years to negotiate with local authorities and the trades unions, but the outcome has been a major improvement in the bus service pattern combined with an extensive degree of inter-working between the operating undertakings.

'Rapidride'

During 1974 Crosville commenced a new service 418/9 between Heswall (bus station) and Liverpool. Known as the 'Rapidride', the service provides the fastest and most comfortable ride to the centre of Liverpool. It is a service which fulfils a Crosville wish of pre-war days to operate services to Liverpool via the Mersey Tunnel. The applications were vigorously opposed by Liverpool,

Bootle, Birkenhead and Wallasey Corporations and in the end did not proceed to a public hearing before the Traffic Commissioners.

The Mersey Tunnel was constructed in tubular form with the roadway cutting through the centre axis of the tube making an upper and lower section, with the intention that trams should run through the lower section. It was largely due to the fact that Liverpool was still developing its tramway system in 1935 when the tunnel was completed, while Birkenhead was scrapping its trams, that this through operation never came to pass. Long arguments were going on right up to the outbreak of war in 1939 between the corporations of Liverpool, Birkenhead and Wallasey, with the Mersey Railway as a critically interested third party. It was because of these arguments that the opposition to the Crosville application was so strong, and that no bus service, even municipal, ran through the tunnel until the advent of the PTE, apart from an emergency service during World War II when the ferries were temporarily closed.

However, a bus service did connect Liverpool and Birkenhead as early as 20 September, 1909 when the Great Western Railway's road motor department introduced a service between Liverpool and Birkenhead (Woodside) GWR railway stations. Three buses were used, and besides calling at various fixed points in Liverpool (as per printed timetable) arrangements could be made to pick-up groups at a pre-arranged originating points. Buses were conveyed across the River Mersey on the luggage ferry boat. The service was not considered successful and it was withdrawn in December 1909.

National Travel

In April 1972 the Central Activities Group of the National Bus Co was established and one of its main objectives was the integration and development of coach operation for marketing on a national scale, which hitherto had been operated either by individual subsidiary companies or by groups working together under joint arrangements. Broadly, this involved the bringing together of various extended tour programmes as 'National Holidays' and development of coach operations for marketing on a national scale. Initially the organisation was based on five companies and in the North West, on the coaching activities of the North Western Road Car Co Ltd which had been reorganised as described in chapter 6. North Western's name became National Travel (North West) Ltd and the services of another NBC coaching company – W. C. Standerwick Ltd of Blackpool – were absorbed into the new company (with its head office at Chorlton Street Coach Station, Manchester) which then assumed control of the services of the other NBC subsidiaries in the region, Ribble Motor Services Ltd, Cumberland Motor Services Ltd and Crosville.

All Crosville express coach services, with the exception of X73, Dolgellau – Swansea, and local ones such as hospital services, were taken into the National network and licences were transferred in 1975, although service 871 between Liverpool and Cardiff has been replaced by the 'Trawscambria' group of services. Since that date numerous changes have been made and new services developed including the 'London Welshman' which commenced operation on 23 May 1976 between Caernarfon and London. Crosville continued to operate many of the services on behalf of National Travel until May 1980, when a National coaching centre was established in Liverpool with an outstation at Caernarfon. This centre took over the actual operation of the services worked from Liverpool, with drivers and administrative staff from Crosville and Ribble.

Coaches for this new unit came from Ribble, National Travel (West) and Crosville (CLL 321 – 5). The chart room is still in Liverpool, but was moved from the Crosville premises at Edge Lane to Skelhorne Street in 1971. Crosville still operates a number of express services on behalf of National Travel.

Bus services in the Oswestry area

Services in the Oswestry area were revised from September 1979 as a result of the data derived from Market Analysis Project surveys which had been commenced there by the company in the summer of 1978. In general the proposed revisions involve an improvement in the facilities offered, including a new service between Sodyllt Bank and Chirk and additional town services in Newtown. Some poorly-patronised services were withdrawn but the changes were made without drastic alteration to the network of bus services in the area.

'Special buses' and service revisions in Wales

'Special buses' have been introduced in Wales, on the one hand for tourism and on the other a 'community bus' to enable residents of sparsely-populated areas to be served by public transport. Snowdon 'Sherpa' is the name by which the Crosville bus service between Llanrwst, Beddgelert and Porthmadog is known. It came into existence as a result of a decision made by the Gwynedd County Council, the Snowdonia National Park Authority and the Countryside Commission to improve tourist facilities in the park. A skeleton service started on 18 July 1976, was stepped-up in 1977 and became hourly in 1978. At Beddgelert another 'Sherpa' operated by O. R. Williams & Son (Whiteways), provides the link with Caernarfon and the coast.

The Uwchaled 'community bus' commenced operations on 28 October 1976. Organised by Crosville and Clwyd County Council, it serves a number of villages in the Cerrig-y-drudion area of Clwyd, linking them with Bala, Corwen, Denbigh and Ruthin. A 17-seater Bedford minibus is driven by a team of volunteer drivers (trained by staff from Crosville's Corwen depot where the minibus is maintained); this team is organised by the Uwchaled Bus Committee, which is also responsible for deciding all operational matters including fare scales and timetables, subject to the approval of the Traffic Commissioners. In the same year revised services were introduced in Central, West and North Wales and during 1977 major service revisions took place in the Rhyl and Deeside areas, to be followed in 1978 by a comprehensive re-organisation of bus services in the Wrexham area and Anglesey. Besides introducing a number of regular 'headways' a 'mini-bus' service using a 16-seater Ford Transit, was introduced, whereby the village of Caim (Anglesey) has public transport for the first time.

Another interesting stage service is the jointly-operated service of Crosville and National Welsh from Cardiff to Bangor. Known as the 'Trawscambria' service, it was inspired as an experiment by the Welsh Office and was introduced in 1978. It qualifies as a stage service by virtue of the fact that on certain sections of the route it conveys local passengers. Dual purpose vehicles in the National Bus Company's coach livery are used but the name 'TRAWSCAMBRIA' is displayed on the sides in place of the fleet name 'NATIONAL'.

NBC Regional structure

During 1977 the NBC regional structure was re-organised again and the subsidiary bus companies were regrouped into four geographical regions, Crosville going into the newly-created 'Wales and Marches' region with South Wales Transport, Western Welsh, Red and White, and Jones Omnibus. For economy reasons the Western Welsh and Red and White companies were merged in 1978 to form a new company which adopted the fleet name 'National Welsh/Cymru Cenedlaethol.'

Transport Act 1978

The Transport Act 1978 added to the Transport Act 1972 the requirement for county councils 'to develop policies which will promote the provision of a co-ordinated and efficient system of public passenger transport to meet the County's needs', and to submit 'Public Transport Plans' for co-ordination. However, a change of government in 1979 has brought a change in transport policy and at the time of concluding this manuscript in Autumn 1980 a new Transport Act had become law; the only provision which had come into effect on 1 August 1980 removed the requirement for conductors to be licensed. This Act is referred to in the next chapter – 'The eighties, outlook uncertain'.

7

The eighties – outlook uncertain

Nineteen eighty would appear to be a repeat of nineteen seventy, with bus companies throughout Britain experiencing reduced numbers of passengers arising from the economic situation of the country. On the other side of the balance sheet costs are escalating as a result of chronic inflation and local authorities are reducing levels of revenue support as part of their programmes to reduce expenditure. As previously mentioned a new transport act came onto the statute book on 1 August 1980 and amongst the various enactments which will be introduced in due course it provides for relaxation in road service licensing, the introduction of operators' licences and the possibility of trial areas where no road service licences will be required. There are a number of other important provisions and broadly the objective is to make it easier for newcomers to enter the industry, thereby increasing the level of public road transport available. In general, stage carriage services under thirty miles in length are protected, but excursions and tours and express services, where each passenger must travel not less than thirty miles, are freed from the necessity to be covered by a road service licence. For the provision of these facilities under thirty miles a road service licence will be required. Is it any wonder that the outlook is uncertain?

The National Bus Company has been carrying out an extensive programme of market research over the last two or three years. This programme is known as the Market Analysis Project, (MAP) and it is designed to produce sufficient factual information related to bus passenger demand and the costs incurred in meeting that demand to enable rational judgements to be made to ensure some stability in the level of service provision and in passenger usage of the services provided. This implies consideration of the three main elements of bus service provision, namely network coverage (ie the route pattern), service quality (frequency, accessibility, reliability, etc) and revenue (ie fares charged).

Crosville has been examining its bus services in close co-operation with the local authorities involved, and having introduced revised bus services in the Oswestry area in 1979 as a result of data collected and analysed through the Market Analysis Project, new schemes of particular interest went into operation during the first months of 1980.

DeCambria

Faced with a 24% cut in Dyfed County Council's transport supplementary grant, savings had to be made in its contribution towards bus (and rail) services in the county. As a result of its Market Analysis Project survey, Crosville was well placed to design a new network of bus services and working in conjunction with the county council revised timetables for services in the Ceredigion region came into operation on 6 January 1980. This scheme achieved major savings in costs with little inconvenience to the public.

Bws Llŷn

The DeCambria scheme was closely followed by a major revision to bus services operated on the Llŷn Peninsula and in the area of Blaenau Ffestiniog. Again survey information provided the basis for the revised timetables introduced on 17 February 1980, which were designed by Crosville with the support of Gwynedd County Council. Considerable simplification of the timetables has been a feature of these revisions.

99

Mid-Cheshire

A week before the Bws Llŷn scheme came into operation Crosville had commenced, on 10 February 1980, a much larger series of changes derived from the Market Analysis Project scheme undertaken in the Northwich and Winsford areas of Cheshire. Titled the 'Mid-Cheshire' network, a name resurrected from the 1920s of a business Crosville nearly purchased (see chapter 1 page 14) the scheme has the backing of Cheshire County Council. To mark the revival of the Mid-Cheshire name, Crosville painted Leyland National SNL386 in a blue-and-cream livery with the title 'MID-CHESHIRE MOTOR BUS CO' on the side panels. During the first fortnight of operation a flat fare of 1p was charged on this bus which ran on different routes throughout the promotional period. A number of special multi-journey tickets have been introduced and from the introduction of the new network all services have been one-man operated. A particularly interesting introduction is the extension of service E66 Chester – Northwich through to Manchester in place of the limited stop service L8/L9, Northwich – Manchester. Whilst operations are centred on Northwich or Winsford as distinct areas, there is a frequent service linking the two towns, and indeed two timetable booklets in blue-and-cream have been printed. In some cases services were reduced, but in many areas services were improved and more journeys added. The Northwich area guide included an advertisement for drivers, together with publicity for the new 'Townride' and 'Interlink' multi-journey tickets.

This series of revisions was closely followed on 15 March 1980 by changes in the area centred on Congleton, Biddulph, Kidsgrove and Tunstall. No identifying name was introduced in this joint Crosville and Potteries Motor Traction Co Ltd (PMT) venture, and whereas green buses of Crosville and red buses of PMT are now found on different routes it is a result of two NBC subsidiaries co-operating to provide the best services in an area in which they both operate. The changes followed a major survey involving Cheshire and Staffordshire County Councils, and whilst certain rural services were reduced a number of services were improved, particularly in the Congleton area where a 'multi-ride ticket' known as the 'Shopride ticket' was introduced together with an 'economy ticket' giving unlimited travel between any two specified bus stops. As a result of the changes Biddulph depot closed and at the same time Congleton opened at the Cattle Market as an outstation of Macclesfield depot. Bus services provided by the Greater Manchester Transport and Crosville are to be revised in the Wilmslow area. Insofar as Crosville is affected, the Manchester – Wilmslow – Alderley – Macclesfield services (E29, E30 and 152) will be diverted in the Handforth area, and the Northwich – Knutsford – Macclesfield services (E25, E26 and E27) recently revised as part of the Mid-Cheshire scheme will be split at Knutsford.

Other bus service revisions

'Hot on the heels' of changes in Mid-Cheshire came a major services revision on Deeside and in Ellesmere Port. Dealing with Deeside first, these broadly affect an area from Chester to Holywell, across to Mold and back to Chester, but bus services operating into the area from Birkenhead, Rhyl and Wrexham were involved. The new network was designed by Crosville and Clwyd County Council and many detail changes took place, some reducing services whilst increased facilities were provided to meet a need identified by the survey data. A new limited stop service, B1X, provides a basic hourly service between Chester and Mold via Broughton and Buckley Cross to Ruthin every other hour. In addition service B4X gives an hourly limited-stop service between Chester and Mold via Saltney and Harwarden, continuing to Denbigh every other hour. The two services between them provide a half-hourly limited-stop service between Mold and Chester rail and bus stations. Numerous changes were made in the Holywell area with the A4 and A5 services between Holywell and Mostyn operating as a circular service on a two-hourly frequency in each direction, but giving an hourly service between Holywell and Maes Pennant Estate.

The trunk Chester — Rhyl services (A1, A2, A3) were reduced from half-hourly to hourly and integrated with the Chester — Holywell service (A7) to provide two journeys per hour over the Chester — Holywell section. From the Chester end buses leave at 25- and 35-minute intervals and from Holywell at 26- and 34-minute intervals. The 'Cymru Coastliner' (Chester — Rhyl — Caernarfon) was unchanged and additional summer journeys from Holywell to Rhyl, on service M27, are to be operated.

In chapter 6 the Cheshire County Council and Crosville public transport plans published in December 1979 were referred to, and on 6 April 1980 revised bus services based on the proposals in the report were introduced. The new network was named 'TransPort' with the object of enabling passengers to identify the new bus services. Housing estates in Little Sutton and Great Sutton received bus services for the first time and Hope Farm Estate was given a direct service to both Birkenhead and Chester through the diversion of service C3. Amongst a number of other service revisions F59, between Ellesmere Port and Neston, was increased to hourly. Of course there were casualties; the withdrawal of F88 Ellesmere Port to Clatterbridge and F96 from Great Sutton to Vauxhall's, while F58 ceased to operate from Chester, its new route being Whitby to Clatterbridge Hospital via Ellesmere Port. A number of consequent adjustments were also made to services 87 and 88 between Birkenhead and Parkgate, and service 89 from Birkenhead to Burton.

Network names

Where a special network name has been introduced buses operating these services carry the new logo on the roof or side panels above the rear wheel arch.

Bus service developments

For the 1980 summer timetable the 'Townlynx' service was extended to serve Manchester Airport four times a day on

Mondays to Saturdays, with a journey time of one hour between Ringway and Ellesmere Port. In addition Ellesmere Port was to be linked to Rhyl on a daily basis with two journeys during the 1980 summer season.

The 'Trawscambria' services has been another successful venture and beside operating on an 'all-the-year-round' basis instead of only during the summer season, the 23 May 1980 saw the introduction of two new routes from Cardiff to Rhyl and from Cardiff to Liverpool to join the highly successful original Cardiff to Bangor service commenced for the summer of 1979. The routes are:

Service 700 CARDIFF – Merthyr Tydfil – Brecon – Newtown – Machynlleth – Porthmadog – Caernarfon – BANGOR

Service 701 CARDIFF – Bridgend – Swansea – Carmarthen – Aberystwyth – Machynlleth – Dolgellau – Blaenau Ffestiniog – Betws-y-Coed – Llandudno – Colwyn Bay – RHYL

Service 702 CARDIFF – Newport – Abergavenny – Rhayader – Newtown – Welshpool – Oswestry – Wrexham – Chester – Birkenhead – LIVERPOOL

Also in Wales, improvements have been made to the Snowdon 'Sherpa' service, but it will be interesting to see whether the economic recession and the down-turn in internal British tourism enables these highly attractive services to be further developed, or retained in their present form into 1981 and beyond.

When the Crosland-Taylor family commenced running its bus services it did so as a means of making money. Life was simple and clearcut: a bus was purchased, put on the road and if through competition or lack of passengers it did not pay, the service was promptly withdrawn. The question of social responsibility did not enter into the calculation, or if it did with some of the larger companies, it was secondary to, or a goodwill feature towards, producing a profit for the owner. A good example of this is Crosville's cross-subsidisation of the Welsh areas based on revenue collected in the English areas.

Conclusions

In concluding this history at a point in time – mid 1980 – it is clear that the evolution and development of Crosville has been a continuous struggle over a period of some seventy years. During that time there have been two world wars, numerous transport acts and a social revolution of which one aspect is the desire of a large percentage of the population to have their own private transport in the form of cars or motor cycles. Undoubtedly the motor-bus following in the wake of horse-drawn stage coaches and wagonettes opened-up the countryside and brought freedom of movement to communities which have remained virtually isolated for hundreds of years. Regular services were offered at reasonable fares and the standards of service and reliability achieved in the 1930s probably represented the industry at its best. Now the wheel has gone full circle; the countryside no longer needs opening-up and has found its own means of travelling to and fro, and the transport industry must seek in the crowded and congested towns new means by which it can offer an attractive service to the community. Gone are the days of evening traffic derived from cinemas, and gone is mid-day traffic when a big proportion of those at work went home for their meal. This has resulted over the last few years in a number of persons who will never own cars theoretically being required to support certain bus services which have no chance whatsoever of paying their way. This social pattern of increasing complexity, coupled with an increasing standard of living and a population which is rapidly becoming too large for the area in which it lives, has rendered the old clear-cut concepts of competition and profit a little out-of-date; it would be a mistake to say that they are no longer applicable but in future, particularly in the realms of transport, they must be coupled with other considerations. Also on the debit side, many roads are unchanged from those available in pre-war days but the traffic flows are much greater, with the result that in some instances bus services cannot offer that degree of reliability which is required. Buses are bigger and the peak travel periods are much more compressed, but Crosville

104

is attempting to overcome all these and many other hurdles in a manner befitting its long tradition as the principal provider of public transport in its operating area.

Organisations that fail to renew their ideas gradually succumb, over time, to those that do review themselves but the innovations in road passenger transport which Crosville have introduced over the last few years would suggest that Crosville 'wheels' will continue to turn into the nineties and beyond.

8

Buses 1910 – 1945

Crosville Cars

Before becoming involved with buses George Crosland Taylor had been interested in motor cars, and in 1902 he had imported from Brussels cars and motor cycles, which he subsequently sold. He visited the Paris Motor Show in 1903, 1904 and 1905, and in 1906 purchased several cars from Monsieur Ville, a chassis, and some drawings. In the end only five cars were produced which ran under the name of 'Crosville' and in 1908–1911 the premises were used for general business as a garage and machine shop. Some work was also done on motor boats.

First buses

With the decision to embark on bus operation a Herald charabanc of French manufacture was purchased second-hand in Swansea but it proved to be worn out, the only replacement parts being available from a similar but scrap vehicle found near Huddersfield. A Germaine wagonette purchased for £50 at an auction at a garage opposite the Grosvenor Hotel, Chester, also proved useless, but the company was eventually successful in obtaining a reliable vehicle when it purchased an Albion charabanc in Liverpool. The late Edward Crosland-Taylor records that 'being determined not to be bilked again, I took it in front of the Lime Street station and attracted a crowd of loafers whom I offered a shilling each to sit in it whilst I tried it with full load up a hill'. This was the vehicle which started the service

106

Above: ECW bodied Bristol LL6B, No KW287 is representative of the number of L types which operated with Crosville. (*Crosville*)

Below: Strachan bodied this AEC Regal (TA9) to standard Tilling design. (*Crosville*)

Above: Concourse of the new bus station at Crewe. The depot entrance is visible at the rear of the manoeuvring area. (*Crosville*)

Below: Double deck coach, ECW/Bristol DFB 111 as new. (*Crosville*)

from Chester to Ellesmere Port in January 1911, during the same year a Lacre was acquired when the Chester to Kelsall service was purchased from Lightfoot Brothers.

At this time Crosville owned a number of other cars, gave driving lessons, hired out chauffeur-driven cars, continued to deal in car sales and repairs, and sold tyres made at Helsby until tyre manufacturing ceased at Helsby Works. Edward Crosland-Taylor recorded the disposal of the final stock:

> 'None of them [were] in such shape that one could guarantee them. I toured North Wales offering these tyres to garages, in an old Wolseley 2-cylinder horizontal delivery wagon that we inherited from the Neston laundry. These tyres required two strong men with crowbars to get them on the rims and I never stayed long enough at any of these garages to hear the remarks of those who had to deal with them.'

The Lacre was followed by a second-hand Herald named *Ella* and two second-hand Dennis vehicles named *Alma* and *Deva*. *Alma* was numbered 2 but was later renumbered 4. Another Lacre (fleet number 3) named *Royal George* came in 1912. This was followed by another Lacre *Grey Knight* (No 9) in 1913, the year in which the company purchased a number of 26-seater Eaton-bodied Daimlers of the CC and CD types. These were later numbered 22-5, numbers 22 and 23 being named *Flying Fox* and *Busy Bee* respectively. Two Tilling-Stevens double-deckers which were numbered 1 and 2 came with the purchase of the business of Ward Bros of Crewe, which had run horse-buses on Crewe town services, while in 1915 two Daimler Y-type 28-seaters numbered 10 and 11 were acquired. World War I stopped a planned expansion of bus services, but the company was busily occupied serving the Queensferry munitions factory for which it needed a fleet of some twenty buses. The factory was visited by King George V, when the vehicles were drawn up in the factory yard for inspection. In 1916/17 eight more Daimlers were acquired, being numbered 8, and 14-20. Of these 19 and 20 were CBs which came in 1916 from the New Brighton Coach Co, 8 and 18 (also CBs) which were purchased new in 1916 and 1917 respectively. Numbers 14, 15 and 16 were new CKs acquired in 1916. The last three buses purchased during World War I were three Lacres numbered 21, 23 and 24, which came in 1917/18. Just after the end of World War I two Rolls Royce cars were purchased and immediately put up for auction at Manchester, but a loss of £25 was made on the deal and no further car sales were entered into.

In those early days drivers had to coax their antiquated vehicles along rather than just drive them. The sprocket drive keys of the Lacres were constantly shearing and the outer sleeves of the Daimlers regularly broke at the lug. Most of the time the brakes were ineffective and the buses had to be constantly driven on their gears. Mr W. J. Crosland-Taylor wrote about some of his experiences with these early vehicles at Nantwich in 1919 in his book *The Sowing and the Harvest*:

> On 19 January 1919, I went to Nantwich, finding four buses there, two Lacres and two Daimlers . . . The Lacres started fairly easily but wouldn't keep going. The Daimlers were more stubborn to start but seldom gave trouble once they were nice and hot. We used to heat petrol in a tin (God help us!) and pour it into the induction taps whilst someone was swinging the engine. This ensured a start, but washed the oil off the sleeves, so it was immediately followed by a dose of engine oil and thus all was well.

On a personal note I can recall, thirty years later, watching four men with a rope, plus one in the cab, trying to start the petrol-engined Titans and Lions on cold Monday mornings. I can also remember flaming rags being placed against the induction manifolds of tired oil engines to get them to fire, and this in the 1950s!

Post World War I buses

The first post-war buses were 25, a 32-seater Daimler CB bought second-hand in 1919; new Daimlers 9,21,3,4 and 29–34; and AECs 26–8. (No 33 with registration No T7082 went to Colwills at Ilfracombe.) Between 1920 and 1923 further vehicles were acquired, amongst them ten ex Royal Flying Corps Crossleys, of which only five received numbers – 1/2/4 and 18/24. A new Crossley (No 3) came in 1920 together with a large batch of Daimlers CKs, numbered 35–48, 50–59 and 100. The last new Daimler CK, No 60, was delivered in 1921 but in the previous year No 49, an AEC 'Y' type had been acquired second-hand. A move of great significance for Crosville occurred in 1921 when two Leyland G7s (Nos 61/62) were purchased, in that no new buses of any other make were purchased for the next seven years, and for the next twenty years Leyland formed the backbone of the Crosville fleet. During the years 1922–3 no less than 51 Leylands were purchased (the new ones costing £32,400), all new except for No 80, a G6B acquired in 1922. The remainder was made up of A7s, A9s, C1s, G6Bs and GH7s, all single-deckers, numbered 8/9, 63–79 and 81–112. Leyland No 72 was fitted with a bigger engine than usual in order to enable it to compete with a Leyland powered with a benzole mixture which was being used by Jim Gibson, with whom Crosville was in competition on the Crewe – Nantwich route. Eventually Gibson sold out in 1923 and with his business Crosville acquired an AEC, a Crossley, a Daimler CK and a Leyland GH7. The 14 buses of J. Pye of Heswall were purchased with his business on 1 January 1924 but soon afterwards seven of them were disposed of. There were five Straker-Squires (Nos 1P–5P), an Albion (No 9P) and a Bristol (No 14P). Those retained were a Tilling-Stevens petrol-electric (No 176), a Pagefield FP (No 177), an Albion N20 (No 178), two 1-ton Fords (Nos 179, 180) and a Tilling-Stevens (No 181). A further Tilling-Stevens was not given a fleet number.

Not every purchase of a business resulted in the acquisition of additional buses but six did come with the business of Richards of Caernarfon (Busy Bee) acquired in 1925. These were two AECs (Nos 197/8 and two Lancia Pentaiota (Nos 199/200) and two Daimlers (a CK No 195 and a CB No 196) acquired with the business of Gauterin Bros of Farndon. As all new vehicles were being delivered with pneumatic tyres it was decided, in July 1925 to convert solid-tyred vehicles as far as it could be done.

New buses in the twenties

Eighty-nine Leylands of various types were delivered in 1924/25 and received fleet numbers 1–7, 12, AC, 14/15, 89, 90, 113–175 and 82–94. Fleet number 13 was not used at this time by Crosville, the Leyland CH7 delivered in 1924 and its successor a Lioness, receiving instead the letters AC.

The year 1926 saw the arrival of the first Leyland LSCI Lions (Nos 201–210) which had Leyland 32-seat bodies. They became A1–10 in the 1935 renumbering scheme and 206(A6) was in use (numbered 43A) until the mid-fifties as a recovery vehicle, latterly based at Chester. The author can recall in the early fifties (as a trainee with Crosville) being asked to drive this vehicle from Liverpool (Edge Lane) depot through the Mersey Tunnel to Birkenhead (Rock Ferry) depot. These Lions were followed in 1926 by twelve 52-seater, open-top, Leyland Leviathans (211–22) and fifteen 36-seater Leyland SG11s (223–37). In 1927 the last SG11s (238–244) were delivered together with 25 Leyland Lion PLSC1s (A11–A35, as renumbered 1935) and Leyland Lion PLSC3s (B46–B51). An additional 46 PLSC3 Lions (B1–B12 and B52–B85) came in 1928 along with nine Lionesses (B13–B21) fitted with United coach bodies. No 276, an ADC '423' delivered in 1928, also had a United body, but this was a bus and seated 35 persons.

In June 1927 several railway companies discovered that some of their main road bridges were not strong enough for heavy vehicles to cross, so beside giving the company both operating and financial problems insofar as they had to divert certain services Crosville had to pay £1,140 to strengthen the bridge at Meols. As payment had also been made to lower a road under a bridge in order to take double-deckers, this may well have been the reason for the notice which appeared in all Crosville bus cabs right into the post-war years, to the effect that 'THIS BUS MUST ONLY BE DRIVEN UNDER OR OVER THE BRIDGES AUTHORISED'.

On 1 May 1929, Crosville was purchased by the London, Midland & Scottish Railway and as a result an AEC Regal with a

21-seater Harrington body, which passed to Crosville was numbered 413 and later became T4, together with an Albion PR28, No 197 (later S9) and two Albion Vikings Nos 411/12 which later became S20–S21. The LMS then purchased three large independent operators in North Wales and amalgamated these businesses with Crosville. The first was Holyhead Motors (Mona Maroon) in November 1929, with 18 buses most of which were withdrawn (one Albion, two Dennis and seven Chevrolets) over the next two years, but eight Albions (1–8) remained to become S1–S8 in 1935. The second business, which came over on 1 January 1930, was UNU of Llangefni ('You need us'; there was a driver at Llandudno junction depot, now retired, known as Bob UNU', who came over with this business, and I am sure many will remember him) and this brought in a further 22 buses of which six Leyland Lions and Lionesses (77–82) became B38–B43, two AEC '424s' became T1 and T2 (previously 85/86). The remainder, ten Vulcans, 89–98, two ADC '416s', 83–84, and two Thorneycrofts (87–88), did not survive to be renumbered into the Crosville fleet in 1935. By far the largest acquisition was the business of Brookes Bros (White Rose) of Rhyl which brought in 87 buses, mostly Leyland, to which Crosville allocated the fleet numbers 414–476. These were a Titan TD1 (414 later L63), five Tiger TS2s (415–9, later K33–K37), eleven PLSC3 Lions (420–30, B86–B96), six Lionesses (431–436, K38–K43), three Leyland Leviathans (437–9) and a collection of older vehicles which were numbered 440–76. The newer vehicles, namely 414–36 all had Leyland bodies. However, fleet numbers were allocated to the remaining vehicles which were AEC (477–80); Lancia (481–88), Chevrolet (489), Fiat (495, 496 and 500), Buick (497), Daimler TM30 (498), Vauxhall (499) and Shelvoke & Drewry (S&D) Low Freighters (490–94).

Fleet renumbering

In 1935 it was decided to abandon the sequential system of numbering and to group chassis by type, each group distinguished by a letter with vehicles in each classification being numbered from '1' upwards. The scheme was arranged as follows:-

A   Leyland Lion PLSC1
B   Leyland Lion PLSC3 and Lioness PLC1
C   Leyland Lion LT1
D   Leyland Lion LT2
E   Leyland Lion LT3
F   Leyland Lion LT5 (petrol)
G   Leyland Lion LT5A (petrol)
J   Daimler CH6, Leyland Lion LT5 (oil), ADC 423
K   Leyland Lioness LTB and Tiger TS (petrol)
L   Double-deckers (petrol)
M   Double-deckers (oil)
N   Leyland Cub normal-control (petrol)
O   Leyland Cub forward-control (petrol)
Q   BMMO, SOS
R   Tilling-Stevens
S   Albion
T   AEC single-deckers (petrol)
U   Miscellaneous

As further vehicle types were purchased, the class system was extended as follows:-

H   Leyland Lion LT7 (petrol)
J   Leyland Lion LT7 (5.7-litre oil engines)
P   Leyland Cub normal-control (oil)
KA   Leyland Tiger (oil)
W   Dennis (petrol) – existing U class Dennis vehicles were renumbered, leaving the U class for Shelvoke and Drewry
S   Bedford and Dodge
WA   Dennis Lancet (oil)
MG   Gardner-engined double-deckers (oil) – existing M class Guys were reclassified
MB   Bristol K6A, K6B – existing Bristol K6As were reclassified, leaving the M class for oil-engined Leyland double-deckers
KB   Bristol L6A, L6B
FA   Leyland Lion LT5 rebuilt with Albion engine
TA   AEC Regal (oil)
GA   Leyland Lion LT5A (oil)
JA   Leyland Lion LT7 rebuilt with Leyland 8.6-litre engines

JG   Leyland Lion LT7 rebuilt with Gardner engines
KC   Leyland Tiger rebuilt with Gardner engines
KG   Bristol L with Gardner engines
KW   Bristol L with Bristol engines – existing KB class Bristol L6Bs were reclassified
MW   Bristol K with Bristol engines – existing MB class Bristol K6Bs were reclassified
OA   Leyland Cub forward-control (oil)
PO   Leyland-Beadle rebuilds from Leyland Cub
SC   Beadle-Bedford
SL   Bedford OB coach
CA   Crossley single-deck
SG   Guy Vixen
UG   Bristol LS6G
UW   Bristol LS6B
ML   Bristol LD6B
SC   Bristol SC4LK
SP   Beadle-Bedford – ex SC class

This system lasted until 1958 when the fleet was reclassified (see page 138)

'Toastracks'

Of these, only 490–92/4 survived to become U6–U9 in the 1935 renumbering. This particular class of bus in the Crosville fleet is of great interest for these 'toastracks', as they became to be named, were based on the chassis of the S&D dustcarts and sewerage disposal vehicles. As originally built they had tiller steering which was operated by the right hand of the driver, whilst his left hand worked the gear lever that controlled the epicyclic gearbox. With very small wheels, these unorthodox buses were only capable of low speeds, but were ideal for summer services along promenades at coastal resorts. In later years the tiller steering was replaced by a conventional arrangement and the driver sat on a centrally-positioned seat. The first Freighter purchased by Brookes Bros of Rhyl was No 71 (DM4833) and was given a 32-seat toastrack body by Simpson & Slater of Nottingham. It was followed by four similar buses numbered 72–5 (DM5266/6233–5). When acquired by Crosville they were numbered 493, 494, 490/1/2 respectively. Their commercial value was obviously appreciated by Crosville, which ordered and took delivery of a further three in 1931, numbered 626–8, also with Simpson & Slater bodies, (FM6459–61, later U10–U12), but in 1932 DM4833 was withdrawn and sold. In 1935 Crosville acquired a further four Freighters U18–U12 (FM9063–6) but this time the bodies built by Simpson & Slater had enclosed sides but no windows. The final batch of three came in 1938 with 32-seat toastrack bodies, built by Eastern Coach Works of Lowestoft (ECW), and as part of a re-allocation of numbers in the 'U' classification, were numbered U12–14 (CFM 340–2) and DM6233–35 were scrapped having been renumbered U1–U3 in the revised scheme of numbers introduced in 1938. The others became U4 (DM5266), U5–U7 (FM6459–61), U8–U11 (FM9063–66). All these buses were stored throughout World War II and ran at Rhyl until 1952 when U6–U10 were sold to Butlins at Pwllheli, where they operated as late as 1961. U5 was scrapped at Rhyl in 1953 and U11 lasted, again at Rhyl, until 1956. The three ECW-bodied Freighters received Bedford, 6-cylinder, 28hp petrol engines in 1955 and operated from that year at Barmouth and Aberystwyth until 1960 when they were sold, minus their engines, to a Warrington scrap merchant. They were driven from Rhyl to Aberystwyth in winter and the route chosen was 'over the Plynlimon road'.

Leylands

All but ten of the new buses delivered in 1929/30 were Leylands – 118 of them. The odd ten were Albion LC24s (later Nos S10–S15) and PJ24s (later S16–19). Of the 118 some 39 were the new Leyland Titan TD1s with Leyland lowbridge bodies. Of this batch 21 received oil engines after World War II and the last one was not withdrawn until 1954. During the early 1950s I did some of my driver training on M225 (TD1) and M569 (TD1 ex-Ribble), both of which had their original bodies and were allocated to Birkenhead, Rock Ferry depot. The TD1s had the accelerator pedal in the middle, as opposed to the right and it was necessary to be careful not to become confused by this non-standard arrangement. One of 1932 Leyland double-deckers M23 (TD2) was the first to complete one million miles, which it did on 25 January 1949 when all the passengers had their fares returned and made their journeys as guests of the company. Another 16 Leyland-bodied PLSC3 Lions Nos 61–76 (B22–B37) came in 1929, together with six Lionesses with United coach bodies 12–17 (K1–K6), twenty-five of the new Lion LT1s 311–24, 339–47 (C1–C25) and eight Tiger TS2s 171–78 (K13–K20). Twelve TS2s came in 1930 and were numbered 348–53, 369–74 (K21–K32) along with twenty-two LT2 Lions which were allocated the numbers 375–96 (D3–D24). Most of these single-deckers were among the first post-war withdrawals but two of these TS2s, K19 and K23, together with a TS3 of 1932 (number K47) all of which had received new ECW rear-entrance bodies in 1939, were fitted with Gardner 5LW engines in 1949 and reclassified KC19, 23 and 47. As such they remained in service until the late nineteen fifties. During their later years they spent time at both Rock Ferry and Crewe depots.

Tyre mileage contracts

The year 1931 saw the company signing its first tyre mileage contract with Dunlop, which bought all the company's tyres, hiring them back at a rate per mile and at the same time organising its own tyre maintenance service in each depot. A similar type of arrangement is still in operation but now with the Michelin Tyre Company.

Second-hand buses and coaches

From businesses acquired in this period only six Tilling-Stevens, taken-over with the North Wales Silver business survived to become R2–R7 in 1935 together with twelve SOS types out of 44 SOS from Llandudno Coaching Co, which operated under the fleet name 'Llandudno Blue'. These were numbered Q1–Q12 in

1935 and all had gone by the outbreak of World War II, except two canvas-roofed SOS 'QLC' charabancs (Q1 and Q2), both of which spent the war years parked in either Llandudno town or Oxford Road depots. I saw one charabanc still in blue in Llandudno town depot towards the end of the war. Both were repainted in Crosville's post-war green-and-cream coach livery, operating on excursions from Llandudno, in 1949. Crosville must have been unique insofar as Tilling group operators were concerned in operating these two charabancs on excursions and tours in the early post-war years. New vehicles delivered in 1931 included three GMCs which it is thought had been ordered by Edwards of Denbigh, and a Daimler CH6 606 (later J1) with a 36-seat United body. A further 40 Leyland Titans of both TD1 and TD2 types, with Leyland lowbridge bodies, were also delivered in 1931/2 and numbered L1–L22 and L64–L81, but the most significant delivery was the forty-first 649, (M1), the first oil-engined double-decker. At that time diesel oil was much cheaper than petrol and in any event the heavy oil engine did nearly twice as many miles to the gallon as the comparable petrol engine. Other petrol-engined vehicles which came in 1931/2 were TS3 and TS4 Tigers (K44–K62) with bodies by Leyland or United; a batch of 49 Leyland Cubs (N1–35 were KP2s and N36–49 were KP3s) with 20-seat bodies by Weymann or Brush and 153 Lions of types LT2, LT3 and LT5, all with bodies by Leyland, Weymann or Eastern Counties. Subsequently the LT2s were numbered D1/2 and D25–52 (plus one un-numbered LT2 FM6479 previously 582 which was burned-out in a fire in 1934), E1–E75 (LT3) and F1–F42 (LT5) and J2 (LT5 with oil engine). These were followed in 1933 by the last Leyland TD2s which had Leyland 48-seat, lowbridge bodies (L82–L86) which were followed by three Titan TD3s with Eastern Counties bodies (M10–12). The final double-decker to be delivered in 1933 was a 60-seat Metro-Cammell bodied AEC 'Q'. Renumbered L87 in 1935 (and later L68) it was number 1000 when delivered. It was used on the Brodie Avenue service which Crosville operated for Liverpool Corporation from 1931–6 and it was sold in 1945. Single-deck deliveries that year consisted of thirteen Leyland

KP3 Cubs (N50–62 with Brush bodies) and twelve KP2 Cubs (N63–74) Brush (N63–8) or Roberts (N69–74) bodies and ten Tiger TS4s with Leyland bus (K68–72) or Eastern Counties coach bodies (K73–77).

Western Transport buses

The acquisition of Western Transport brought in a further 133 vehicles but only the 49 Tilling-Stevens B10As and B10A2s with 32-seat Brush bodies (R8–R56), four Morris Rs (U13–U16) and one ADC 423 (J3) survived to be renumbered in 1935. The remainder, which included nine ADC 423s, twenty-nine Daimlers, sixteen Maudsleys, nine Dodges, seven Thorneycrofts, five Chevrolets and four Guys were disposed of. Very few vehicles were retained from the large number of operators acquired in the mid-thirties, although a number of Leyland Lions and Tigers from the fleet of Seiont Motors of Caernarfon were absorbed as A36, B97, C26/27 and K87/89. The two Ks were included in a batch of vehicles (K13–37, K44–7, and K88–9) rebodied in 1936/7 with ECW 32-seat bus bodies. From the coach fleet of Macdonald came ten AEC Regals with Duple or Massey bodies, which became T6–T15, and survived until 1952–3, although in 1939 they had received new ECW rear-entrance bodies with 32 coach seats and were operating in the Rhyl and Llandudno area. Pearson, Jones and Horn contributed four AECs (T16–19) including a Q type (T19). The other three were treated in a similar manner to T6–T15 and received new bodies, while their four Leyland Tigers became K93–K96. New double-deckers were M2–M9, Leyland TD3s with Leyland or ECOC, 52-seat bodies. In 1939 K8–12, K42–3 (ex Pritchard 1936), 46–62, and K93–4 received new bodies.

Other new vehicles at this time consisted of a large number of Leyland Cubs delivered in 1934/35. Some nineteen were of the KP2 and four were of the KP3 type with Brush 20/6 seat bodies numbered N75–N97. Twenty were forward-control SKP3s with Brush 30-seat bus bodies (01–020) and two were SKP3s with Harrington 26-seat coach bodies (021–22). There were twelve normal-control KP02s with 20-seat bodies of which P1–P6 were bodied by Tooth of Wrexham, whereas P7–P12 had bodies by Brush. 012 was fitted in 1949 for a short time with an oil engine and renumbered 0A12. A large number of Lions also came at this time, LT5As with 34-seat ECOC or Leyland all metal or Tooth bodies (see Appendix IV) numbered G1–G21, oil-engined LT7s with ECOC bodies, numbered J4–J28, and a further group of LT7s with 32- or 34-seat Leyland all metal bodies, numbered H1–H15. In the early post-war years the Gs and Js were rebodied by Burlingham and ECW respectively, given Leyland 8.6-litre or Gardner 5LW oil engines and reclassified GA, JA or JG as appropriate. Twenty-five petrol-engined coaches were Leyland Tiger TS6s numbered K78–K86 (new in 1934) and K90–K92 which came in 1935 to be followed in 1936 by TS7s Nos K97–K10, with bodies by Duple, and Harrington and TS7 No K109 (ordered by Pritchard) with Burlingham body.

Maintenance problems

There was concern in 1935 in regard to the state of the fleet. Maintenance of vehicles was cut to three farthings per mile and much essential work had been left undone. It is evident that the extensive deliveries of new vehicles were a help in containing maintenance costs but problems with timber-framed bodies had become serious. Many buses were suffering from dry rot, usually in the side pillars at joints and over the wheel arches. At first the joints were reinforced with metal plates but this was not successful. Pressure washing, the use of steam-dried timbers in the construction, and age all took their toll. In June it was decided to have new bodies for 105 of the Lions and some of the Lionesses rebuilt to forward control; the work was put out to tender with the result that the contract went to ECW. At the same time a body shop manager was appointed, together with some additional body builders who started work on 'in-company' body rebuilds. At this time engines were rebuilt by Leyland Motors at a rate per mile, Crosville having very little machinery in their repair shops.

The KAs and Ms

KA1–15, the first of the legendary Leyland oil-engined TS7s and TS8s with 32-seat bodies by the Eastern Counties Omnibus Co Ltd were delivered in 1936. (The body building side did not become separate until later in 1936 when it was named Eastern Coach Works Ltd – ECW). In 1949/50 they received new Saro bodies by Saunders Roe of Anglesey (except KA11 which was rebodied in 1943 with a Burlingham 35-seat body) and featured a destination blind which had an outside flap to blank off the opposite destination, the intermediate points being common to both displays. They were then all allocated to Rhyl and Denbigh depots. Double-deckers delivered consisted of Titan TD4s with Leyland all-metal or ECW bodies numbered M13–M21 and M41–M46 (M19–21 were TD4s with torque converters and Leyland all metal bodies). The gap was filled by nineteen of the 'L' class TD1s and TD2s, which received oil engines in 1935 and were renumbered M22–M40. These were followed in 1936 by twelve Leyland KP2A Cubs with 20-seat Brush bodies (N98–N109) and in 1937 by twenty-two KPZ01s and KPZ02s with Brush 20-seat (P13–24) and 26-seat (P25–34) bodies. These were the last Cubs to be purchased. Coaches continued to be petrol-engined and in 1937/38 Crosville took delivery of twenty Leyland TS7s and TS8s with Harrington bodies numbered K1–K6, K38–K41 and K110–K115 and no less than seventy-two KAs, with 32-seat front-entrance ECW bodies, numbered between KA16–KA87; KA27 had a detachable postbox fitted on the nearside rear panel and for years operated the Llandudno – Eglwysbach service.

Forty-two Leyland TD5 double-deckers (M47–M88) with 52–seat ECW bodies came in 1938–9 and six of these (M71–M76) had removeable roofs for summer working as open-top buses. At first they ran at Llandudno in the standard maroon-and-cream livery, but in post-war years were all at Rhyl in an overall cream livery. M88 was the first double-decker to cross the rebuilt Menai Bridge into Anglesey on 26 March 1945 en route from Bangor to Holyhead. In the nineteen forties and fifties most of the buses received extensive body overhauls and were re-trimmed. Apart from receiving the standard Tilling front destination indicator, their outward appearance remained unchanged. WA1, a Dennis-bodied Lancet 11 and three Dennis (W1–W3), came with the acquisition of the business of Lloyd of Bwlchgwyn in May 1938. A further 66 KAs, numbered between KA88 and KA153 arrived in 1939.

Ribble sold twelve Lions of the PLSC1 and PLSC3 types to Crosville in 1939; these were renumbered A31–A40 and it is interesting that all but two (A31 and A37) of the PLSC1s were later lengthened to PLSC3 and renumbered B15–B18 and B38–B40. During the later years of World War II some of the Bs received semi-austerity bodies. The last petrol-engined Tiger to be delivered was K116 a TS8 with a Burlingham coach body. Further KAs with ECW 32-seat bus bodies were KA154–KA165 but KA169–KA171 (also delivered in 1940) received new secondhand ECW bodies from K37/4/5. Most of these were allocated to the Rhyl and Llandudno division, and KA148–65 differed from the earlier KAs in that they had an additional indicator over the first window adjacent to the entrance door. Burlingham put coach bodies on three of this batch of chassis which were numbered KA166–KA168. In addition to the single-deckers further Titan TD5s with ECW bodies numbered M89–M100 were acquired. Additional new Leyland double-deckers were ten TD7s diverted from East Kent numbered M101–M110. These were also allocated to the Rhyl and Llandudno division and M102 was, with KA28, amongst the first vehicles to be painted green in 1944. Another sixteen TD7s were diverted from Southdown and numbered M111–M126. They had highbridge bodies but several of this class were allocated to the North Cambrian division and based at Bangor and Caernarfon depots. Ten more TD7s came in 1942 with 'unfrozen' chassis and utility bodies by Brush, Roe, Willowbrook and Northern Counties; they were numbered M127–M136. Incidently, in 1939 Crosville had placed an order with Leyland for 102 new chassis, which included 66 double-deckers.

Wartime deliveries

Other new vehicles to be purchased during the war consisted of 21 utility Guys, delivered in 1942–3 and 15 Bristol K6As (M171–84, M186–87) with Strachan 55-seat bodies, delivered in 1945. They were followed by seven similar vehicles in 1946 (M185, 188–92), the same year in which they were reclassified 'MB'. The Guy Arabs were numbered M137–M157 and had Gardner 5LW engines (except for M147/148/153/157 which had Gardner 6LW engines) They were reclassified MG in 1946. Their lowbridge utility bodies were by Roe, Northern Counties and Brush (M153–7 had slatted wooden seats) and all were allocated to the Crewe division where they remained until withdrawn in 1955/56. A Leyland Tiger TS3 was obtained in exchange for N45 from Thames Valley and numbered K117. Arising from the establishment of armaments factories in the company's area and other wartime requirements for public transport, Crosville faced a shortage of buses and a large number were hired from other operators. They came from a variety of undertakings, some from Manchester Corporation, the Caledonian Omnibus Co of Dumfries and a variety of other sources. At the end of the war their owners wanted them back, and Crosville entered the second-hand market, purchasing double-deckers at prices ranging from £25 to £1,200 each. The first second-hand acquisition was seven Titan TD2s from Bolton Corporation and eight similar from Plymouth Corporation. Two TD1s came from Exeter and six from Leigh Corporation. There was a Lion LT2 (D3) from West Yorkshire and six Regents from Brighton, Hove & District. These had outside stairs and ran as such until 1948 when the bodies were scrapped, the chassis overhauled and fitted with new ECW lowbridge bodies, the completed buses being numbered MA601–MA606. One of the Manchester Corporation buses operated on hire to Crosville during the war appeared in the victory procession held in London on 8 June 1946, when it still carried the Crosville fleet identity to mark the fact that it had run with Crosville during the war years.

Wartime ambulances

During 1939 thirty-two single-deckers were converted into ambulances for ten stretchers each and held at the disposal of the Ministry of Health for air raid casualties, while a number of the E and F class single-deckers had their seats arranged along the sides in order to enable them to carry 30 standing passengers. They become known as the thirty/thirties. Thirty-eight vehicles, mostly coaches and 20-seaters, were requisitioned in April 1941. One had an experimental five-speed gearbox and after a great deal of struggling, Crosville got it back in exchange for another one. In 1942 experiments were carried out with gas-powered trailers in order to meet a government requirement to save fuel, and after visits to Eastern Counties and Eastern National to see trailers in operation. 101 were ordered at £100 each. However, only about fifty were in operation when the instruction was cancelled. Wear and tear was heavy with the trailers and the unused units were cannabilised in order to provide spares. Petrol-engined Leyland Tigers based at Chester, Rhyl, Wrexham and Crewe were chosen but it is believed that most of the operation was concentrated at Wrexham. At the end of the war all the trailers were sold for £13 each. Repairs and maintenance of buses during the war became very difficult and there was a continual shortage of spare parts and skilled labour. A new innovation in 1943 was the introduction of advertisements on vehicles.

Fleet livery

The first Crosville buses were grey but in the twenties it was changed to LMS maroon, with a cream roof. To this was added at a later date cream bands under the windows, and on double-deckers a cream band around the centre line of the vehicle. These bands were outlined in black and the company name and fleet number was displayed in gold. In 1944 the livery was changed to green, and for a time buses appeared painted in two shades of green, darker above the middle of the vehicle and lighter green

Above: The late
W. J. Crosland-Taylor,
MC, MInst T, shortly
before his retirement.
(*Crosville*)

Below: CRG 162, an ECW
bodied Bristol RELH6G
loads passengers at Birkenhead, Woodside, in 1972.
(*Crosville*)

Above: Seddons on the Runcorn busway. Note the fare box to the left of the gear lever. (*Crosville*)

Below: ERG 598 operating on the Cymru Coastliner, climbs past the now demolished Craigside Hydro. Llandudno Bay and Great Orme is in the background. (*Crosville*)

below with cream bands and black lining. This soon gave way to standard Tilling green-and-cream, and the gold lettering was continued until 1954, when it was retained for fleet lettering but small, black plates with the fleet numbers in silver replaced the gold letters and numerals. KW94 was among the first, if not the first, to be so treated. The black bands on repainted vehicles disappeared about this time, but for a time new vehicles were still delivered lined-out in black. M54 sported an all-green livery for a time in 1953, but it did not find favour and the central cream band was restored. The cream band under the windows on double-deckers did, however, disappear. Single-deckers with standard ECW bodies had the window surrounds painted cream, as did the upper deck windows of double-deckers with ECW bodies for the first deliveries after World War II. They never had a cream band under the lower deck windows, which was a feature of the previous buses, and this was omitted from such buses as and when they were repainted. However, the first TD7s to be painted in green in 1944 did feature such a livery but it was shortlived. Occasional variations did occur and, when many of the KAs had their bodies overhauled, they lost their cream band in favour of cream around the window pillars. There was a reversion to the cream band with the introduction of the ECW-bodied Bristol LSs, but there were variations with dual-purpose vehicles which have appeared in all cream, and then later a green-and-cream livery. During the early 1960s a revised gold fleet name appeared. It was smaller and used capital letters of the same size. This was followed in 1971 by large transfers using lower-case lettering, the first buses so treated being the Seddons. In 1973 the standard NBC livery of green with the NBC logo was introduced.

In pre-war days coaches were grey-and-green with some cream relief, but as a result of experiments carried out in 1944 coaches began to appear in a livery of cream-and-green which was retained until they were sold. However, the first post-war coach KB1 was painted cream-and-green, as were the dual-purpose bodies of this type used on various new and rebodied chassis. The LWL6B coaches commencing with KW231, were cream overall with a thin green line between two pieces of aluminium strip at the lower edge of the body, and green wings. The ECW-bodied LS and MW coaches had cream bodies, with the window surrounds painted black, as did the ECW-bodied RE coaches. They retained this livery until they received, as appropriate, the overall NBC white paint scheme.

As I have mentioned above there were occasional variations to suit individual vehicles and the Bedford SLs had cream bodies with green roofs, semi luxury Lodekkas ML675–ML682 were all cream with black window surrounds and wings, but Lodekkas DFB109–113 and DFB149–53 used on the Liverpool–North Wales express services and later on as the 'Cymru Coastliner', were cream overall. The latter had illuminated off-side advertisement panels featuring Crosville publicity.

During the war years the edges of the wings, dumb irons, lifeguards and other vulnerable areas were painted white to assist in greater safety during the blackout, bearing in mind the restricted lighting permitted in the vehicle itself.

9

Post-war buses

Post-war vehicles

With the end of the war the company could forsee the expansion in traffic which was to be a feature of the late forties and early fifties, but the fleet was in a sorry state after six years of war, with its attendant difficulties. W. J. Crosland-Taylor in his book *State Owned Without Tears* wrote: 'The life blood of a bus company is its vehicles, they are more important than anything else . . . they earn the money that keeps us going, gives us our living and buys every single thing we use'. New vehicles were not immediately available and the policy of buying second-hand continued, with the result that in 1946 thirty-one Titans of types TD1–TD4 with various bodies, came from such diverse undertakings as Bury Corporation, Ribble, Sheffield Corporation, Chesterfield Corporation, West Riding and Western SMT. Another twenty-two second-hand Titans were obtained in 1947, including one built in 1946 which was obtained from LCW Motor Services in exchange for KA168 and N94. This Massey-bodied PD1 was numbered M520 and allocated to Rhyl depot where it worked on the service to Llandudno. The balance was made up of one petrol TD1 and two petrol TD2s from Rawtenstall Corporation, eight TD4s and TD5s from Chesterfield Corporation, five 'unfrozen' TD7s from the Western SMT, and five TD1s from Wigan Corporation. The first new double-deckers to arrive were Leyland PD1s M521–539 which were allocated to the Rhyl and Llandudno division, and PD1As M540–M555 which went to the North

Cambrian division. All the new PD1s and PD1As had ECW bodies, but a batch of eight PD2/1s, numbered M583–M590, diverted from Cumberland Motor Services Ltd to Crosville in 1949 (and registered HRM etc), had Leyland lowbridge bodies and were allocated to Llandudno and Llandudno Junction depots. Seventeen further PD2/1s with Leyland highbridge bodies (and registered by Crosville as new) numbered M592–M600 and M610–617 were all allocated to Rhyl depot. When ML661 was delivered in 1953 M613 was loaned to Chester depot and these two vehicles ran on similar bus workings on the service to Birkenhead for fuel consumption tests. The only other new Leyland vehicles was a batch of thirty-five Tiger PS1s with MCW bodies (diverted from Midland General), first licenced on 1 January 1950. Numbered KA225 – 259 they were at first painted in bus green-and-cream, being allocated to Rhyl and Llandudno and North Cambrian divisions. Subsequently they saw service at Wrexham, Merseyside and Crewe and later they were painted all cream and used on express services. A number had low-ratio back axles fitted for the Liverpool – Pwllheli service.

Other non-standard vehicles delivered at this time were twelve AEC Regals (TA1 – 12) with Strachan 35-seat bodies, built to standard Tilling design. TA1–4 went to Chester, whereas TA5–12 went to Rhyl and Llandudno. No new coaches had been built since 1939 and there was a government order prohibiting building new bodies for coaches. When this was rescinded the first new coach was KB1, a 31- (later 32-) seat Bristol L6A, with bus body and coach seats. Painted cream with a green flash on the side panels, it operated when new on the Liverpool – Caernarfon service. However, the first new coaches in 1945/50 were petrol-engine Bedfords with Duple bodies, numbered SL30–76. Two of these (SL51/52) were transferred to Tilling Transport (BTC) Ltd, London, which returned two similar coaches JXH649/50 (also numbered SL51/52) to Crosville in 1953. Petrol thefts were a problem, but red dye in the petrol and the very severe penalties put a stop to petrol thefts from bus tanks. As well as providing chassis for coaches Bedfords supplied in 1947/49 a batch numbered S2–17 and S20–24 which had Beadle 28-seat bus bodies. These buses had a short life with Crosville, being sold to a private operator in Ceylon (now Sri Lanka). In 1972 the son of the purchaser – by then an employee of the State Transport undertaking – was attached to Crosville for management training. A variant of this body, but lengthened to carry 35 passengers, was developed as a chassisless vehicle and in 1949 two, SC18 and SC19, (in later years they were re-numbered SP18–SP19) were based on Bedford running units. When withdrawn from stage carriage operation they became mobile enquiry offices. They were initially allocated to Llandudno Junction depot, but in later years SP18 was allocated to Rhyl and SP19 went to Anglesey. Another twenty similar vehicles, numbered PC13–PC32, were constructed, in 1950 using running units from Leyland Cubs (P13–15 and P17–33). The PCs were very unpopular with drivers but for a time worked on the Llandudno – Caernarfon service.

Bristol/ECW vehicles

Other divisions of the company were receiving ECW-bodied Bristols of standard Tilling design, the first going to Merseyside. Standard K6As and K6Bs delivered between 1946 and 1950 were numbered MB/MW251–417. At first all were numbered MB, even those with AVW engines, and it was not until a number of these vehicles were in service that the necessity to distinguish engine types brought the new suffix 'W' into use (Appendix IV). Contemporary Bristol single-deckers were KB/KG/KW1–116 and were of L6A, L6B and L6G types. Later the AEC engine was not used in the Bristol chassis, and these buses were numbered KG/KW117–164, KG/KW175–229 and KW269–KW293. Most of the vehicles in higher numbers (from SLG150) were of the LL5G, LWL5G, LL6B or LWL6B derivatives. KG193–KG203 had 8ft wide bodies on 7ft 6in chassis, whereas KWs 274–293 were 7ft 6in wide LL6Bs. With standard ECW bodies the 'L' types seated 35 passengers and 'LL' or 'LWLs' seated 39. The earliest 'L' types (up to the 80s) had a side destination indicator over the window in front of the rear entrance door, but this was never used. MWs 384 and 385 were allocated to Newcastle-under-Lyme depot and worked the service to Crewe and Chester until displaced by Lodekkas. The author took his first steps as a driver on KWs 271, 272 and 273, subsequently taking his PSV test on MW492. Among the single-deck chassis was a batch of LL6Bs and LWL6Bs which received the standard ECW, 35-seat coach body. Delivered in 1951 and numbered KW230–KW268 they were magnificent vehicles and worked, as befitted them, on the Liverpool–London service. KW230–44 had 8ft 0in bodies on 7ft 6in chassis and in 1958 the whole batch became CLB230–68.

Further deliveries between 1951 and 1953, before the arrival of the Lodekkas, were a substantial number of KSW6Bs and one KSW5G. Numbered MW418–27, 429–99 and 631–60, they were mostly of the lowbridge type with the exception of MG428 (KSW5G) and MW429–442 which had highbridge, 60-seat bodies. MG428 was allocated when new to Chester, MWs 429–38 were at Rock Ferry and MWs439–42 were at Wrexham. MWs 418 and 419 were allocated to Liverpool, Edge Lane and had five-speed gearboxes. For a time they worked the Liverpool to Warrington service via Cronton and Farnworth. KWs 165–74 were L6Bs with standard ECW bodies, but painted cream with a green flash and fitted out with 31 (later 32) coach seats. Of the K6As delivered in 1949 some thirty were diverted to London to deal with a shortage of new buses in the capital, and did not arrive at Crosville until 1950.

Summer 1948

The acquisition of new vehicles meant that some of the older vehicles could be scrapped, although the Tilling-Stevens single-deckers (Rs) had to be used in the summer of 1948 as there was an operational requirement in the summer of that year for 1,246 buses. (In summer 1950 the highest ever requirement of 1,334 vehicles was operated).

First withdrawals

The question of vehicle replacements was of paramount importance and in August 1949 it was decided to scrap 300 single-deckers, replacing them with as many double-deckers as could be found. The traffic department endeavoured to get as many routes as possible authorised for double-deck operation, whether or not the buses were immediately available, and so it was that many buses which had opened-up bus routes for Crosville, then served throughout the war, were withdrawn from service and scrapped. Petrol prices were increasing and petrol vehicles returned a lower mileage per gallon than those with oil engines, so it was obviously petrol-engined vehicles out first, beginning with the As, Bs and Rs, then the Cs, Ds, Es, Fs and Hs, with the result that by 1949 72 had been sold; in 1950 it was 153, in 1951 only 93, 103 in 1952, which left 127 petrol-engined buses in the fleet – mostly Bedfords. There were also six Lion LT3s (E7/14/33/52/61/68) which had been cut down to waist level in 1951. Nicknamed 'boats' they operated seafront services in North Wales (mainly Rhyl) until withdrawn in the late fifties.

Rehabilitated vehicles

Meanwhile, the majority of the petrol-engined Titans received new oil engines between 1944 and 1946 and most of those purchased second-hand received similar treatment. Many double-deckers received new standard ECW lowbridge bodies, and whereas some retained their original short radiators, others received new, deeper radiators. A number of Tigers was fitted with oil engines from 1947 onwards, several had new bodies, and many were rehabilitated as described in the previous paragraphs. Whilst the earliest KAs (KA1–10/12–14) were rebodied by Saunders-Roe of Anglesey with rear-entrance bodies and a unique destination indicator which featured a spring-loaded flap to display the terminal destination, a number in the range from KA16–87 (Appendix IV) had their sides rebuilt, but most of those in the higher number groupings remained in the

133

original state to the end, except for their interior trim. Crosville buses, when maroon, had dark mahogany woodwork, red leather seating, or cloth with a dark red pattern with red leather trimming. When buses were re-trimmed, and this applied to numerous KAs, double-deckers, and others, the woodwork was replaced or repolished in a teak shade and the red leather was replaced with green, whilst the cloth was a red/green mixture on a fawn background. A completely overhauled, re-trimmed and repainted KA was quite a magnificent sight. Most Leylands had their manufacturer's radiator plate substituted with one with the single word 'CROSVILLE', a practice which had lasted from pre-war days, but this arrangement did not extend to the post-war Leylands.

A rehabilitated Lion which had a special history was F18 which had its original body destroyed in the fire at Rhyl in 1945. It was rebuilt as FA1, having been equipped with an Albion oil engine and an Eastern Counties body from ECOC Ltd DE11. F8 also received a new Albion oil engine and a new ECW bus body in 1949.

Some pre-war Metro-Cammell, double-deck bodies were obtained from Salford Corporation in 1952 and one of these was mounted on a chassis built up from the remains of an ex-Birkenhead Corporation TD4 and a K–type Tiger. (M639) Crosville then established a design for its own highbridge bodies and whilst three of the ex-Salford bodies were fitted on the chassis of a number of Titans obtained from Sheffield Corporation, four of this same batch of chassis received new Crosville bodies in 1953. Similar Crosville bodies were mounted on the majority of TD7s diverted from East Kent and Southdown during the war and also on one of the 'unfrozen' TD7s delivered new in 1941. In 1953 new ECW bodies were fitted to the chassis of the 1945/46 batch of 22 Bristol K6As in place of the Strachans utility bodies, some of which were scrapped, while six were mounted on a similar number of the 15 Bristol chassis acquired from the London Transport Executive in 1953 and numbered MB160–70 and MB193–6. (Appendix IV). At the same time as the wartime K6As had new bodies their radiators were replaced with those standard on the post-war 'K' type Bristol chassis. The vehicles were easily recognisable by the rounded back axle hub as opposed to the 'squared-off' post-war version. Other ex-London K6As received post-war ECW bodies from MA series AECs as they were scrapped.

There were also five open-toppers which came second-hand in 1950 from Brighton, Hove & District and were renumbered MA608/9, 618–20. Another ex-Brighton AEC (MA607) had been purchased in 1948. Further second-hand Titans and AEC had been obtained in 1948/9, many others coming via Bristol Tramways second-hand from Exeter Corporation and Wilts & Dorset (two AECs and five TD2s). Others were three TD2s from Cardiff and an exchange with an operator named Jones of N52, N60 and WA1 for a TD3 and a TD4. A further five TD2s were bought from East Yorkshire Motor Services Ltd. Ten Leyland Tiger KAs were exchanged (see appendix iv) in 1952 for ten Leyland Titan TD1s of Wilts & Dorset. As most had Gardner 5LW engines the numbering was M640 (8.6-litre Leyland engine) and MG641–9. Some of the buses operated in Wilts & Dorset red/cream livery at Rhyl and Crewe for a short time. As a result of the purchase of an independent, a Crossley (CA1) and a Guy Vixen (SG1) were in the fleet for a short time. MGs 621–26 were AEC Regents with Gardner engines and MG 627–30 were Bristol GO5Gs obtained from the Brighton Co in 1951. Of these MG629/30 were painted cream and used as 'open-toppers' at Rhyl.

Lodekkas

The acquisition of second-hand double-deckers ceased at the end of 1953, the year in which the first pre-production Lodekka, ML661, joined the fleet. One had been on trial with Crosville in 1950, and after much testing with other Tilling companies the final design had evolved. All the first Crosville Lodekkas had AVW engines, and deliveries of production models commenced in 1953. There was still an acute shortage of double-deckers during the early part of the 1954 summer season, and for a few weeks a number of Warrington Corporation double-deckers operated on hire to Crosville on the Birkenhead – Chester service. ML675–82 delivered in 1954 only seated 52 and were painted in an overall cream livery with black window surrounds. Fitted with two card tables in front of the rear facing bulkhead seats, they had coach seats and were initially used on the Liverpool – Llandudno Junction express service, but later went to the Newcastle – Chester service, but without the tables. In later years they were painted in the half-green, half-cream style of the express fleet. Over the years Crosville took into stock 593 of these buses with Bristol chassis and ECW bodies, commencing in 1953 with ML661 (an LD6B) and ceasing in 1967 with DFG263, a FLF6G with semi-auto gearbox and Clayton heaters. The group is made up as follows:

Type	Total
DLB	257
DLG	95
DFB	124
DFG	117

Most of the early DLBs had no rear platform doors and had a platform of normal design, but later deliveries had rear doors. (see Appendix IV). However, a number of these buses came built for platform doors with rear platform emergency exit, but without folding doors which were installed at a later date. DLG811–18 and DLG977–82 as built had detachable tops for promenade services and were painted cream. DLG797 was destroyed by fire in December 1965 and rebodied by ECW in 1966. After experimental work on DLBs 844 and 845 all Lodekkas from DLB899 onwards received Cave-Brown-Cave heaters. DLG949 was the Bristol LDX flat-floor prototype.

The highest number reached was DLB990 and the next deliveries in 1958 commenced at DLG1 and the numbering continued through to DFG263. The first FS chassis delivered were DFB23–5 and FLF DFB40–53 in 1960. Other deliveries were as follows:

FS	DFB/DFG	26–39,	119–49,	154–98,	204–38
	60 seats	1960	1962/3	1964/5	1966
FSF	DFB/DFG	54–83			
	60 seats	1961/2			
FLF	DFB/DFG	84–108,	114–18	199–203	239–63
	70 seats	1961/2	1963	1965	1966/7
	55-seat	109–13	149–53		
	DD coach	1962	1964		

In December 1977 Bristol Omnibus loaned nine FLF6G vehicles to Crosville to replace Lolines at Warrington. These were BOC 7046/7/9–55. Although 7050/1 were soon returned, the remainder were purchased in spring 1978 and became Crosville DFG746/7/9/52–55. DFG746/7 spent time at Chester whilst DFG755 went to Biddulph and later became Crosville's MAP survey bus. By April 1980 only DFG747 remained. DLG871/6/8/944/946 and DFG 68/81 were converted to open-top for the summer of 1977 together with DLG1 which ran with 'top on' at Rhyl for that season. Vehicles now used are permanent open-tops which are only licensed in the summer, ie DFG68, 72, 81 and DLG1, 813, 814, 817, 876, 878, 944 and 946.

The double-deck coaches DFB109–13 and DFB149–53 were originally used on the Liverpool – North Wales express service and on the Cymru Coastliner. Painted cream when first built, in due course the panels below the lower deck windows were painted green. However, when coaches were painted into National white the vehicles continued to be used as duplicates on express services but painted in NBC green bus livery. Later they were used on stage services, mostly Caernarfon – Llandudno and the last survivors of this interesting group of buses ended their working life on school services in the Bangor area.

Fleet numbering

In 1958 the fleet numbering scheme was changed to one in which the classification is made up of a group of letters:

Type of vehicle

S – Single-deck
   (Green livery)

E – Single-deck
   (coach in green/
   white livery)

M – Minibus

C – Single-deck coach
   (white)

D – Double-decker
   (lowbridge)

H – Double-deck
   (highbridge)

Type of chassis

Single-deck

L – Bristol L, LL, LWL
   (later Bristol LH and
   Leyland Leopard)

M – Bristol MW

R – Bristol RE and
   Bedford CF

S – Bristol SC

U – Bristol LS

C – Commer

N – Leyland National

P – Seddon

T – Ford Transit

V – Bedford VAM

Double-deck

K – Bristol K, KSW

F – Bristol Lodekka FS,
   FSF, FLF

L – Bristol Lodekka LD

A – AEC Renown

D – Daimler Fleetline

E – Dennis Loline III

V – Bristol VRT

Type of engine

A – AEC

B – Bristol and
   Bedford 340

F – Bedford VAM/66D
   also Ford

T – Bedford VAM330D

G – Gardner

P – Perkins

L – Leyland

Note: Some of these classifications are now obsolete.

As a consequence of this arrangement the KW/KB/KG class became SLB/SLA/SLG/CLB/ELB. MW/MB/MG became DKB/DKA/DKG, UG became CUG/EUG/SUG/CUB/EUB/SUB and ML became DLB. Earlier vehicles which were unlikely to be retained in the fleet for any length of time were not renumbered, although the Leyland single-deckers became ETEs (Leyland PS1s, later STEs) the double deck PD1s, DTEs, and the PD2s DTOs. The remaining AECs (TAs) became SRAs.

Post-war liveries

The first post-war Bristol ECW double-deckers had the top deck window pillars painted cream, but this practice soon ceased and all deliveries had the two cream bands on a background of Tilling green. Some vehicles, including the Leyland PD2s, had a third cream band below the lower deck windows. In the early nineteen fifties the black lining of the cream bands was discontinued on repainted buses, but new vehicles continued with the arrangement until it too was deleted.

Open-top buses were painted cream, and when the open-top Lodekkas were delivered they had the lower deck window surrounds and pillars painted black, another practice which was to cease with repainting. Later these buses were to go into National white, with the Crosville fleet name in red, and in 1980 those at Rhyl had the fleet name followed by '50 YEARS IN SUNNY RHYL', to mark the takeover of the Brooks Bros (White Rose) business.

In the mid-sixties a larger and attractive gold fleet name began to appear on stage vehicles. This featured all the letters in lower case, apart from the 'C' of 'Crosville'. Some coaches featured a central green band but all this was overtaken with the introduction of the National Bus Company's standard liveries. Although dual-purpose vehicles featured the livery whereby the lower panels were green and the window pillars and roof all buses, both single- and double-deck at first, did not include any white relief with the green, but in due course the white band was incorporated in the paint scheme. At the time of writing, however, single-deck stage vehicles were again appearing in all-green livery. Coaches were repainted in National white and bear the fleet name in red. All buses and coaches have grey wheels and some of the exceptions to the standard livery arrangements for special purposes are mentioned elsewhere in the chapter. Buses based at Heswall, Liverpool, Rockferry and West Kirby depots display the Merseyside PTE emblem and the NBC logo.

Single-deck buses and coaches

Following on from KW293 the first underfloor, horizontal-engined, Bristol/ECW LS coaches delivered in 1952/3 were fitted with Gardner 6HLW engines (UG294 – UG323), but the second batch of seven, which arrived in 1953, had a horizontal version of the Bristol AVW engine and were numbered UW324–30 (CUG/EUG/CUB/SUB/EUB 324–30). 325 was rebodied in 1958 after an accident and re-registered 752 GFM. 302 received a new body in 1957 and 300 had a new bus style front fitted in 1958.

No further single-deck buses were taken into stock until 1956 when ten LS6Gs with ECW 41-seat bodies were purchased. Numbered UG331–40, later SUG331 and EUG 332–40 only UG331 was a bus, the remainder being dual-purpose vehicles. They had a mainly green livery with a minimum of cream relief, but they had coach-type seats. Later they were painted all-cream, with green relief in place of cream. A similar livery situation applied to many of the buses delivered over the next few years until the predominantly cream livery was established in the mid-sixties.

The LSs were followed in 1958 by a batch of 20 Bristol MW6Gs, all of which were dual-purpose apart from the first of the series which was a coach – CMG341. Bristol MWs with ECW bodies continued to be delivered through to 1966 and both buses and coaches were numbered consecutively from 341 to 492; 497 – 523; 533 – 570; 581 – 592; and 30 – 36. In all there were 103 SMGs, 100 CMGs and 33 EMGs. For classification see Appendix VIII.

Whilst the LS chassis was designed for integral construction with all bodies being manufactured by Eastern Coach Works, the MW chassis was a heavier unit designed for separate body construction. With regard to bodywork, the coaches seated 39 passengers and the first 31ft long vehicles were CMGs 467 – 92. Dual purpose vehicles (EMGs) seated 41, and the SMGs to 451 had similar capacity but were subsequently upseated to carry 45 persons. Over the years there were numerous conversions arising from accident rebuilds, changed requirements, and so on. As an example, CMG341, 357–70, 386–90, 407–14 which seated 39 as coaches, were converted to SMG buses and received seating for forty-three. Coaches numbered CMG427–36 and 467–90 were also converted to buses but remained at 39 seats. All the LSs were withdrawn towards the end of the nineteen sixties and the early seventies, at the end of which the MWs started to be withdrawn from service, the last being sold early in 1980. SMGs 363/5, 376, 390, 394/6/8/9 were transferred to United in the summer of 1976.

Towards the end of the nineteen sixties twelve Bristol LS6Gs with ECW 45-seat bus bodies, dating from 1953/54, were acquired from Red & White and United Welsh. These vehicles were SUG282 – 91 from Red & White on 30 November 1967 (LAX632, 635, 640, MAX 101, 103, 105, 106, 107 and 124) and SUG292, 293 from United Welsh in 1968 (JCY 998, 999).

Lightweight single-deckers

In due course, vehicles with different chassis and engines were to be delivered and the first of these were sixteen 35-seat Bristol SC4LKs built in 1957/8. Originally numbered SC1–20 (as a result Bedfords SC18/19 became SP18/19) under the reclassification scheme they became SSG601–20. Further deliveries were SSG/CSG621–79 and between 1957 and 1961 seventy-nine of these vehicles were purchased and they were numbered SSG for the bus version (35 seats) and CSG for the coaches (33 seats). All had ECW bodies and SSG664 had an experimental, all-plastic/fibreglass body. The last SC4LKs

(SSG674/5) in passenger service were withdrawn on 20 March 1976 as a result of the cessation of service M94 which passed through the upper gate in Conwy's town walls. SSG612 survived until the latter part of 1979 as one of the Runcorn 'busway' maintenance vehicles (G612); it was then purchased for preservation.

Bristol REs

During the early nineteen sixties the Bristol RE chassis was developed. This had the engine at the rear as opposed to the 'amidships' arrangements on the LS and MW chassis. The first Crosville REs were a batch of RELH6Gs built in 1963 with ECW 47-seater coach bodies and manual gearboxes, numbered CRG493–96. Painted cream with a black waistband, they were soon followed in 1964 by nine similar coaches numbered CRG524–32, and in 1966 by CRG571–80. These coaches had the high floor, but ERG593–8 RELL6G which came in 1966/7, had ECW dual-purpose, 50-seat bodies; only 596–8 had semi-automatic gearboxes, although ERG1–6 which also came in 1967 were RESL6Gs with semi-automatic gearboxes, and being of a shorter length only seated 42 persons and were used on the Wrexham – Barmouth rail replacement service. A batch of RE buses with semi-automatic gearboxes also came in 1967; these included SRG7/8 which were standee variants with seating for 36 and standing for forty. Originally they had experimental fibreglass seats. SRG7 was withdrawn in 1971 following fire damage. SRG9–22 were conventional 53-seaters, but SRG23–5 were RESL6Gs with seating for 46. Four RELH6G coaches numbered CRG26–9 were also delivered in 1967.

Rebuilds and withdrawals

Before listing further new vehicle deliveries it is appropriate to record that by the early nineteen sixties all the pre-war and post-war Leylands had been withdrawn, and by 1965 the first of the Bristols had also gone. These included the KW buses and coaches

Above: Leyland National in all green livery and equipped for fare-box operation. (*Crosville*)

Below: Ex North Western Park Royal bodied AEC No DAA 504. (*Crosville*)

Above: Ford Transit mini-bus in operation in Anglesey. (*Crosville*)

Below: Plaxton bodied Leyland Leopard No ELL503 in special Town Lynx livery. (*Crosville*)

KB1, KW165–74, and some of the early MBs, MWs and KGs, although several were retained as tow vehicles or tree-cutters. Two other elderly buses in the fleet at this time were SP18 and 19, renumbered MO18 and 19 and used as mobile offices.

The situation was such that by 1964, for a period of about one month, the fleet was composed of all Bristol chassis with ECW bodies. Most of the remaining L type Bristols (but not the LLs or LWLs) previously fitted with rear entrances, had been modified in the company's workshops with front entrances and equipment for one-man operation. In addition, a smaller destination indicator layout was adopted on the Ls and a number of the Ks.

Later REs

A considerable number of RE buses and coaches (all with ECW bodies except where stated otherwise) were taken into stock between 1968 and 1973, amongst them were CRG37–41, 47-seat coaches dating from 1968. Buses and dual-purpose vehicles which came in that year were SRG42 – 51 (53-seaters), SRG62 – 71 (48-seaters with twin doors) and ERG52 – 61 with coach seating for 50 passengers. A batch of 46-seat RESL6Gs numbered SRG72 – 101 arrived in 1968, to be followed in 1969 by ten RELH6G, 47-seat coaches numbered CRG102–111. The final five RELH6G coaches with fleet numbers CRG 160 – 64 came in 1970, but in the meantime SRG 112 – 27 (53 seats) and SRG 128 – 43 (48 seats, with twin doors) had been taken into stock during 1969. Sixty RE buses were purchased in 1970 (SRG165 – 84, 205 – 24 with 53-seat bodies, and SRG185 – 204 with 48-seat, twin-door bodies); SRG225 – 32 are RESL6Gs with Marshall 43-seat bus bodies, new in 1968 to North Western Road Car Co Ltd and acquired by Crosville in 1972. Further RELLs which came with the North Western takeover had Leyland engines and were SRL233 – 37 (Marshall 49-seat bodies), SRL238 – 46 (low-height, ECW 49-seat bodies), and SRG247 – 58 with conventional ECW 49-seat bodies. Ten Leyland-engined RELH6L coaches, numbered CRL259 – CRL268, entered service in 1972, and of twenty-four 50-seat dual-purpose RELL vehicles which arrived in 1972/73, ERG269 – 88 had Gardner engines and ERL289 – 92 had Leyland engines. Plaxton provided the 47-seat coach bodies for CRL293 – 302, ten RELH6Ls of 1973, but it is fitting that ECW should have provided the 47-seat coach bodies for the final batch of nine RELH6Ls, numbered CRL303 – 11 which were new in 1974.

SRG213 (replacing EPG724) has been converted to take 10 seated passengers and eight wheelchairs which are loaded by a hydraulic ramp through the lower back door. By early nineteen eighty most of the first REs were withdrawn from service, including a number with semi-automatic gearboxes.

Bristol LHs

Replacements for the SC4LKs were Bristol LHs, of which sixteen were delivered in 1969. These had Eastern Coach Works 45-seat bodies and as this variant had a 6-cylinder Perkins engine; the chassis description was LH6P with fleet numbers SLP144 – 59. All have now been withdrawn. The first eight vehicles had 7ft 10in wide bodies.

No further new LHs were taken into stock until 1975, when forty LH6Ls, (SLL641–70 with Leyland engines) and Eastern Coach Works, 43-seat bodies entered service. Originally intended for Midland Red, they were diverted to Crosville in exchange for 20 Leyland Nationals. All of these buses are allocated to the three Welsh divisions. The 1976 order called for twenty-two LHs, which however were diverted to other NBC companies as follows: Northern General 6; Eastern Counties 4; Eastern National 4; Trent 4; and United Counties 4. Crosville's 1977 vehicle programme included thirty LHs, whilst the 1978 programme provided for forty, however, the order was exchanged for a similar number of 10.3-metre Leyland Nationals SNL 641 – 70.

In June 1978 Crosville purchased twelve LH6Ls from United Counties (UCOC 400 – 412), dating from 1969 and 1970. These were numbered SLL987 – 99 by Crosville and the last examples survived until early 1980.

Rear-engined double-deckers

The first rear-engined double-deckers were 19 Daimler Fleetlines with 75-seat Alexander bodies, acquired with the takeover of the North Western services in 1972. Numbered DDG301 – 19 (301–302 built 1963; 303 – 13 built 1966; and 314 – 19 built 1967) at the time of writing those remaining in service were DDG304 – 5, 308, 310 – 12, 315 – 17, 319. Recent further acquisitions of Daimler fleetlines, in 1980, were purchased from Southdown: HDG900–14, TCD370J–384J with Northern Counties highbridge 71-seat bodies, built in 1970 and HDG915–29, XUF385K–399J with ECW highbridge 74-seat bodies, built in 1970.

Crosville's first new, rear-engined, double-deckers consisted of twelve Bristol VRT/S12/6LXBs with ECW 74-seat bodies numbered DVG264–75, delivered in 1975 and followed in the same year by eleven VRT/SL3/6XLBs with similar bodies numbered DVG276–87 (DVG284 had a fully-automatic gearbox). The 1976 delivery of six VRT/SL3/501s (DVL287–92) had Leyland engines, and all deliveries of Bristol VRTs since have had Leyland engines as standard, the latest being DVL444. Further deliveries in 1980 had Gardner engines, DVG445–65 having been delivered. Additional vehicles to DVG499 were awaited. During the summer of 1974 Crosville borrowed nine Gardner-engined, Bristol VRTs from Potteries (PMT 610–18) which became Crosville DVG610 – 18. These were delivered new with Crosville fleet names, were painted green, and allocated to Liverpool, Edge Lane depot. These stayed with Crosville until late 1975; however, in the summer of that year 611 and 612 were returned to Potteries and Ribble Leyland Atlanteans 1301 and 1369 were loaned in their place. Early in 1980, six 1972 East Lancs-bodied VRTs with Gardner engines (OWE 267/72 – 4/7/80K) were purchased from South Yorkshire PTE and numbered DVG11 – 16, later again reclassified HVG 931–936.

Non-standard double- and single-deckers

As part of the North Western takeover, Crosville became the owners of eleven Dennis Loline III, DEG401 — 11, built in 1961/2 with Alexander 71-seat front-entrance bodies. Together with the fourteen AEC Renowns with Park Royal 74-seat front-entrance bodies (DAA501 — 16) all these vehicles were withdrawn in 1978 and 1979, the AECs going last. A large number of single-deckers were also amongst the buses transferred, and although these were all withdrawn by September 1975 their fleet numbers were: Leyland Tiger Cubs STL901 — 16, Leyland Leopards ELL917 — 29; AEC Reliances SAA985 — 88, EAA989/990, SAA991 — 95 and EAA996 — 99. In 1974 995/999 were transferred to PMT for spares.

With the takeover of the Western Welsh depots at Newquay and Newcastle Emlyn on 23 April 1972, Crosville acquired eleven Leyland Tiger Cub single-deck and dual-purpose vehicles. Renumbered STL930 — 40 by Crosville, they dated from 1956 (STL930) to 1966 (STL940). STL930 had a 44-seat Weymann body. STL933 a Metro-Cammell body, 940 had a Marshall body, whilst 931/2, 934 — 9 were bodied by Park Royal. All these buses were withdrawn by July 1976, but in the meantime Crosville had acquired from South Wales Transport two ex Western Welsh Willowbrook-bodied, AEC Reliance 41-seat, dual-purpose buses (SAA 983 — 4) which were allocated to Aberystwyth. These had been withdrawn by the end of 1974.

In connection with rail-replacement bus services in North Wales, Crosville took delivery in December 1964 of two Commer 11A minibuses with Perkins engines and Harrington 12-seater bodies. Numbered SCP1 and 2, these buses are now withdrawn. Further 'non-standard' vehicles acquired in 1967 were ten Bedford VAM5s (330D engine) with Duple (681 — 86), 45-seat and Plaxton (687 — 90) coach bodies numbered CVT681 — 90. Four further Bedfords, this time VAM70s (446D engine) with Duple 45-seat coach bodies and numbered CVF691 — 94, arrived in 1969. By 1980 several of these Bedfords had been taken out of service and sold.

Of all the non-standard vehicles owned by Crosville in recent years, perhaps the most unusual purchased were 100 Seddon RUs with Pennine bodies, built in 1971 and 1972. Fifty were numbered EPG701 – 50 and operated as dual-purpose buses (equipped with Webasco heaters) with seating for 47 passengers. The other 50 were allocated fleet numbers SPG751 – 800, and fitted with twin doors have seating for 45 persons. Another Seddon built in 1974, with Pennine 7 body and 49 seats (numbered SPG699) was later added to the fleet. From late 1974 until the autumn of 1976 the Seddon demonstrator SPG700 (ABU451J) was operated at regular intervals.

EPG724 was converted to allow the carriage of wheelchairs, until it was returned to standard layout when replaced by Bristol RE No SRG213. A number of the Seddons (SPGs) have been converted from twin-door to single front entrance and 'upseated' to 51; however, a number of Seddon buses have now been withdrawn from service.

As a complete contrast, two 1976 Ford Transits with 16-seat bodies (in NBC poppy red livery) numbered MTF700/1 are allocated to Corwen and Bangor depots. A further minibus was purchased in spring 1980 (MRB702) a Bedford CF340 with a 17-seater Reeve Burgess body in poppy red livery.

Perhaps the most dramatic non-standard bus is XEB461. This experimental prototype bus is a standard Leyland National single-decker converted to run off lead acid batteries carried in a trailer. Passenger capacity remains unaltered. The design and conversion was undertaken by another NBC subsidiary, Ribble Motor Services Ltd of Preston, in conjunction with Bosch of Germany and British Leyland. This bus has been in use on the Runcorn busway since 9 December 1975 in NBC poppy red livery. A Wadham-Stringer Vanguard 29-seater front-entrance Leyland Cub demonstrator was used early in 1980.

Leyland Leopards

Crosville's first Leyland Leopards were a varied collection of 13 which came from North Western and were collectively numbered

CLL917 – 29; some were re-numbered and reclassified in the series ELL317 – 29. They had a mixture of Alexander and Plaxton 49-seat coach bodies and were built between 1963 and 1966; of these only ELL317/20 – 2 remain as towing vehicles L317/20 – 2. Five 1963 Marshall-bodied 53-seater buses on Leopard chassis (SLL941 – 5) were purchased in 1972 from the Yorkshire Woollen District Transport Co Ltd for use on the Warrington, Altringham and Urmston group of services.

New Leopards in the shape of seven 49-seat Plaxton-bodied coaches numbered CLL312 – 18 arrived in 1976 followed by another batch of nine Duple 49-seater coaches in 1977 (CLL319 – 27). However, CLL321 – 25 were transferred to National Travel (West) in early 1980 (in connection with the establishment of a National Travel coaching unit at Liverpool), and some Leopards have been reclassified ELL. During 1978/9 Crosville took delivery of a further batch of ten Duple-bodied Leopards (ELL/CLL328 – 37) followed by similar vehicles ELL/CLL497 – 511 in 1979. About the same time, six 1970 Leopards with 47-seater Plaxton bodies were acquired from National Travel (East), equipped for use on stage carriage services, repainted into dual-purpose livery and numbered ELL517 – 522.

Leyland Nationals

A batch of 24 Leyland National dual-door 44-seaters numbered SNL801 – 24 entered service in 1972, to be followed in 1973 by a further 70 of which ENL825 – 69 are dual-purpose, 48-seaters and SNL870 – 94 are 49-seater single-door stage carriage vehicles. Another 18 of the 48-seater dual-purpose vehicles (ENL 895 – 912) arrived in 1974, followed by 66 similar buses in 1975, which received fleet numbers ENL913 – 78. In 1976 a further eight 49-seater single-door buses numbered SNL979 – 86 entered service. ENL899/934 have been withdrawn due to structural and fire damage respectively.

The next deliveries of Nationals were numbered into the 300 series with SNL340 – 57 arriving in 1978, with a batch of 49-

seater vehicles diverted from Ribble (SNL358 – 98) in 1978/9 and a further 19 in 1979 (SNL399 – 417).

Crosville's first batch of 30-series B 10.3m Leyland National 44-seater LH replacements, arrived in 1978 (SNL641 – 70) with a further 45 following as SNL556–600, and in 1979/80 ten more (SNL671 – 80). Ten Leyland National series B scheduled for Crosville were delivered to South Yorkshire PTE in National green in early 1979, and the batch for Crosville was re-scheduled for later delivery.

Temporary loans

A number of interesting vehicles have appeared on Crosville routes on loan from other companies in addition to those already mentioned, and those which were acquired to provide spare parts. In the winter of 1973 North Western (by then part of National Travel (North West)) loaned five Alexander-bodied coaches (239 – 43) for use at Northwich. During the spring of 1974 Western National (Royal Blue) loaned six Bristol MW coaches, of which 2255/6 went to Corwen, 2261/7 to Chester and 2243/63 went to Crewe, while Northwich operated North Western Alexander-bodied Leopard coaches 155/6 and 162.

September 1974 saw perhaps the most unusual loans when five Southdown Leyland PD3/5 with Northern Counties full-width fronts, forward-entrance bodies were 'hired in'. Numbers 917 and 914 were used at Macclesfield while 932, 938 and 950 went to Rhyl. Also at Macclesfield were five Harrington-bodied Southdown Leyland Leopard coaches, 1703, 13, 15, 17 and 30. Number 1713 also spent some time at Crewe. For several days Lincolnshire MW bus 2077 operated in Runcorn after having been substituted for a failed coach on express work. Acquisitions for spares have included Lolines from Greater Manchester, Fleetlines from Potteries and an AEC Renown from East Yorkshire.

10

Premises

Depots

Crosville's first premises were Crane House, Crane Wharf, Chester, and an associated warehouse rented from the Shropshire Union Railway & Canal Co in 1906. A small machine shop was installed in the warehouse, and between 1906 and 1908 a new workshop was built across the access lane to Crane Wharf, this forming the nucleus of the repair shops which were used, as such, until 1953. These warehouses had become disused in the mid-eighteenth century as Chester's importance as a port diminished, and it was with delight that the Shropshire Union Canal Co obtained a tenant, albeit at a low rent.

In 1915 a garage was built at Nantwich; it had a span of about 32ft and would hold nine buses. A 1-gallon Bowser petrol pump and a 1,250-gallon tank were installed, and this was a great improvement on the previous arrangement whereby buses had been parked in the Cocoa House yard and refuelled by external filling from tins which were stored in a 'petrol pit'. At the Cocoa House the office was part of a stable. During 1923 a garage was opened at Mold and in January 1924 the purchase of Pye's business at Heswall brought with it a large amount of land in the centre of the town. The additional waiting room, toilets and covered platforms resulted in one of the first bus stations in the country, opened by Crosville in 1924. Other garages on the Wirral at New Ferry and West Kirby had been opened in 1923. The year 1924 saw the establishment of a garage at Barmouth acquired from a Sydney Beer who owned a laundry there.

Claude Crosland-Taylor had leased a large plot of land adjacent to Crane Wharf for 75 years from Chester Corporation, which eased matters as Chester depot buses were operating from an open yard adjoining the repair shops. Warrington depot was also opened in 1924, to be followed in 1925 by the establishment of premises at Aberystwyth and Llanidloes, the same year in which Crosville opened at Caernarfon. The following year saw a new depot at Blaenau Ffestiniog, and at Chester the site of the old roller skating rink in Upper Northgate Street opened as a depot in 1927, in which year Criccieth depot was established. Part of the Loggerheads Estate was purchased in 1926 at an auction sale in Mold for £1,600. This was a favourite beauty spot some three miles from Mold. Crosville eventually built a tea-house on the site which could accommodate parties of 100 people or more and the adjoining woodlands were opened to the public. In the summer there were bands and free entertainments, while on 2 June 1928 an Eisteddfod was held on the site.

A depot at Queen Street, Crewe, was opened in 1926 to be followed by Liverpool, Edge Lane and Llandrindod Wells in 1928. During 1929 arrangements were made to park buses in an open yard at Aberaeron, on the edge of the river running into the harbour. This site was affected by floods and in 1948 a new depot and office was built to house about eight buses, on a site about 100yd from the stand. A surplus army steel-framed building was used, and this became Crosville's first post-war depot. The purchases of the businesses in North Wales brought in the depots at Rhyl and Denbigh in 1930, at Llandudno Junction, Llandudno (Town and Oxford Road), Llanrwst and Bangor in 1931, and at Wrexham, Johnstown and Oswestry in 1933.

Holyhead depot had been established in 1930 with the purchase of the Mona Maroon business, and at Llangefni in 1930 with the acquisition of UNU. Also in Wales, depots were built at Pwllheli, Aberystwyth, Dolgellau, Corwen and Machynlleth in 1934 and at Amlwch in 1935. They were mostly built of asbestos sheeting or Robertson's patent metal cladding rather than brickwork, to keep down construction costs.

In 1936 it was decided to build a depot at Flint. The company had hoped to acquire some land near the railway station owned by the LMS, but in the end obtained a site half a mile outside the town on the road towards Rhyl. Flint depot was opened in 1937 and about this time land was purchased adjacent to Caernarfon depot which had been established in 1932, the same year as the present Rock Ferry depot was opened.

At the same time as the land deal in Caernarfon took place a house on the Square was leased and there Crosville set up a cafe on the ground floor with the divisional headquarters upstairs, which is still in use as such. The present depot was opened in 1936. In 1948 Criccieth depot was closed and its activities transferred to Porthmadog, where buses had been run since 1936 from a shed with no office or fuel pump. All cashing-in, refuelling and traffic returns were done at Caernarfon, Pwllheli or Blaenau Ffestiniog depots and an inspector based in a small office in Porthmadog generally supervised the operations. So another ex-army building, this time a hut, was produced and erected as a temporary building on some railway land and this, together with a fuel storage tank inside the shed with a pump by the door, constituted Porthmadog depot. This, of course, was the time when new Leyland PD1A double-deckers operated what was then service 539 between Caernarfon and Porthmadog – often with full loads and standing passengers. In June 1937 extra land was purchased at Liverpool, and towards the end of that year it was decided to enlarge the depot at Mold.

In 1938 Crewe Corporation promoted a Bill which, amongst other things, provided for a bus station to be located not far from the Square. At this time the Bill was opposed and to secure its passage the bus station clause was dropped but after World War II the idea was resurrected. It was on 21 June 1960 that this fine modern bus station was opened with adjacent depot and as a result the divisional offices at the Square and the depot in Queen Street were closed. Nantwich depot was also closed in 1962. The two other depots in the Crewe division were at Middlewich (which was established in 1934 and closed late in 1972) and at Newcastle-under-Lyme where arrangements were made in 1932 for Crosville buses to be housed at the PMT garage in Liverpool Road. This is now an outstation of Crewe depot.

During the World War II a field at the back of Mold Road depot at Wrexham was laid with macadam to provide open air parking for nearly 150 buses. During the winter hot water in tar boilers was provided in an effort to keep vehicles warm. At this outside parking area it was often necessary to drain the radiators each night in winter, but I can recall at Rock Ferry in the fifties that buses were parked in rows, two rows being radiator to radiator with coke burning braziers at strategic intervals to prevent water freezing.

During the war years Rock Ferry depot was twice damaged by bombing, once from a land mine which exploded in the field behind the boundary fence and secondly from an incendiary bomb. Until 1941 canteen facilities had been available in Liverpool, but these premises were destroyed in the air raids of May 1941 and since that date a mobile canteen had been placed at the Pier Head stand during the day. Something bigger was needed and eventually arrangements were made in 1942 to rent from the GWR a damaged house in Irwell Street. Repairs were made and proper canteen facilities restored at these premises which stood out like an oasis amongst other war damaged properties. Just after the end of the war in Europe the Crescent Road depot at Rhyl caught fire on the night of 16/17 July 1945. It was completely destroyed, and with the building had gone 13 buses in the ensuing conflagration. Buses from all over the Crosville system started arriving at Rhyl in the early hours of the morning and eventually 60 were parked in the streets near the depot; on the morning following the fire no services were lost.

Crosville opened one new depot during the war, in 1942, at Runcorn to serve 42 buses. The original depot had been established at West Road, Weston Point in 1920 and by 1935 eight buses were garaged there with one parked at a funeral director's yard. In that year a local operator's business was acquired and with it a garage and petrol station in Baker Road. By 1939 the fleet at Runcorn had increased to 29 of which twelve were parked at the ICI complex. The new depot at Broadway was on a site which consisted of land made up with waste from soap manufacture and the building suffered from structural problems. It soon proved inadequate, and additional parking space was provided in a large yard adjacent to the garage. The redevelopment of the town of Runcorn which was confirmed by the Runcorn New Town master plan of 1966 that incorporated the Runcorn 'busway', brought about as a logical consequence the establishment of another new bus depot at Beechwood Avenue, Runcorn, in place of the premises at the Broadway. This new depot was officially opened on 30 November 1975, operations having commenced from there on 23 November 1975.

During and just after World War II Crosville purchased a number of houses in the vicinity of Crescent Road depot at Rhyl. Originally the idea was to develop the site into a combined garage and bus station and at about the same time some land (subsequently sold) was purchased in Old Colwyn as a site for a garage. The Town and Country Planning Act 1947 prevented these schemes going ahead, although a rear entrance was eventually constructed for use by buses entering Crescent Road which was used in the summer as a garage for the sea front service buses and coaches. By day the premises were (and still are) used as the setting-down and picking-up point for express coach services, the depot and workshops for Rhyl being at the Albion Works premises. Of the houses, some were converted into flats for staff and two became hostels for summer staff, many of whom came from Queen's University, Belfast, who used to hold notorious parties from time to time, particularly at the end of the season. The author recalls visiting the hostel one summer's day to inform the occupants that, as a result of complaints received from householders in the vicinity, it would be desirable if no end of season party were held that year, to which he received the reply 'To be sure we understand Mr Anderson, but will you come!' The best house on the corner of West Parade and Prince Edward Henry Street was made into the main tours booking office. A further plot of land was purchased in Warrington as a site for a future bus station but this again was baulked by the Town and Country Planning Act 1947. Perhaps the most disappointing purchase was the six-acre Vicarage site in Wrexham, acquired by Crosville in 1944, for which Sir Giles Gilbert Scott (the architect who designed Liverpool Cathedral) was to design a super bus station for Crosville. But Wrexham Corporation would not agree and in due course compulsorily bought the site, in return leasing the King Street bus station to the company for a long term of years commencing in 1952. Because of the inability to obtain planning permission, land which Crosville had purchased as a site for a possible depot in Old Colwyn was sold to Meredith & Kirkham Ltd (motor dealers) who owned the adjoining property.

Continued movement of buses in and out of garages, and particularly on open parking areas, quickly destroys the hard standing unless it is well constructed. Many of the parking areas were more or less flooded in winter, and it was a great improvement when in 1949 the work of laying them in concrete was undertaken at Chester (Sealand Road), Mold, Flint, Crewe, Wrexham, Liverpool and Birkenhead. At Liverpool there were problems as the depot is on the site of an old ropeworks, and it was necessary to dig down 9ft in some places to get a solid foundation. The office and waiting room at Heswall Bus Station were extended to make a depot office and staff canteen, while in the winter of 1953/54 the open part of the High Street Bus Station at Rhyl was covered in. In February 1950 Llanidloes depot was opened, only to be closed on 24 June 1972 when it became an outstation of Oswestry. Johnstown depot closed on 13 May 1972.

Crane Wharf office and Sealand Road works

In 1935, shortly after the new body shop had been opened, it was decided to buy more land at Sealand Road with a view to establishing at some future date a Central Repair Works on the site, and this was the situation when World War II commenced in September 1939. By 1942 Vickers-Armstrong was using two of the bays for the manufacture of aeroplane components and in that year asked for the use of a third bay, pointing out that the firm would be in serious difficulty if not allowed to use it. Crosville retorted that it was equally important to keep the buses on the road, otherwise essential workers could not get to the factories. The outcome was an arrangement whereby the Ministry of Aircraft Production (MAP) agreed to build two extra bays with MAP and Crosville sharing the cost, but providing for Crosville to eventually purchase the second bay at an agreed price. When in 1943 the work was completed, Crosville obtained a brand-new paint shop, twice the size of the old one, and later all the property came into the company's possession.

With the body shop located at Sealand Road it was necessary for loads to be transferred between there and the chassis side at Crane Wharf. Lister trucks were used and it was obvious that to have the two premises in the same location would be a great advantage. The offices at Crane Wharf were most unsatisfactory, ventilation and heating were poor, and being largely constructed of timber, they were a fire risk. In 1949 it was decided to move the machine shop as soon as possible down to Sealand Road and to convert the building into offices. The work of conversion was undertaken by the company and the new offices were occupied in November 1950. In March 1950 approval had been received for the reorganisation of the Central Repair Works but it was not until 1953 that it came fully into use, with the result that the old erecting shop in Crane Street could finally be vacated. One winter this was used to house the intake of new Lodekkas and the author can well remember the morning in 1954 when the drivers converged on Chester from their various depots to collect them. Bus after bus moved out of the doors – there must have been 40 to 50 vehicles housed in the building, which was subsequently let to the Merseyside and North Wales Electricity Board.

Llandudno closures

As part of reorganisation in the Llandudno area, the Mostyn Broadway depot was closed in June 1971. It is now used as a motor car sales showroom and filling station. There were two offices in Clonmel Street, Llandudno; one has been closed and the former tours office modernised and retained. The Oxford Road premises have also been closed and the premises sold. Express services now use Mostyn Broadway coach park, and parking for coaches is provided at the municipal coach park, Builder Street.

Ellesmere Port

An office was opened at Ellesmere Port bus station in April 1972, the bus station had opened on 9 September 1962.

Chester bus station

For many years Crosville had wished for a bus station in Chester, but it was not until 1972 that one was provided by Chester Corporation as part of the development of the city centre. On 18 December the premises, flanked by Delamere Street and George Street, were opened by the chairman of the North Western Traffic Commissioners, C. R. Hodgson, OBE, FCIT. The new bus station was built to deal with all bus and coach services coming into Chester, with the exception of local bus services provided by Crosville and Chester Corporation.

Prior to 18 December 1972 Crosville bus services in Chester had terminated at the Market Square (Town Hall), Delamere Street and Lower Bridge Street. Whereas the local services continue to pick-up in the Market Square adjacent to the Town Hall, they use a terminal point in Delamere Street in close proximity to the bus station, which is of modern design. Access to the buses is through a series of screens along the front of the concourse directly onto the bus forecourt. These screens have been designed to allow passengers to pass through easily and yet to keep out the inclement weather. The passenger concourse is provided with overhead radiant heating and along the rear of the concourse passenger amenity facilities are provided.

Other new facilities

During 1974 improved maintenance facilities were provided at Llandudno Junction, Macclesfield and Warrington, followed in 1975 by major depot improvements at Chester and Liverpool. A bus station was opened at Oswestry on 18 January 1976, and in 1980 Crosville commenced to use the newly-opened municipal bus station in Warrington.

Former North Western, Western Welsh and South Wales Transport depots and outstations

As part of its share of this NBC subsidiary Crosville took over in 1972 the depots at Northwich, Macclesfield and Biddulph. The last-named depot was closed early in 1980, and at the same time Congleton was opened at the Cattle Market as an outstation of Macclesfield. Also in 1972, on 23 April, the Newcastle Emlyn and New Quay premises of Western Welsh and Lampeter outstation of South Wales Transport were transferred to Crosville.

11

Administration

Although Crosville was operating buses before and during World War I, it is generally considered that the developing bus business really got under way just after the war – in 1919 to be precise. With the financial guidance of George Crosland-Taylor it was Claude Crosland-Taylor who guided the destinies of Crosville between 1911 and 1929, succeeding his brother Edward Crosland-Taylor. Expansion plans in 1919 brought about a situation whereby W. J. Crosland-Taylor joined the business, and it was arranged that Claude Crosland-Taylor would look after the head office side of the business with W. J. Crosland-Taylor being responsible for the outside operations of the company.

Departmental organisation

As early as 1911 the company had engaged a chief engineer – Wally Wright – and he remained with Crosville until 1939, but it was not until 1930 that Crosville had a full-time accountant when Herbert Eckersley joined the company from the LMS. As the company had expanded the experience of the early days, with very small fleets, freedom of fares and timetables and little clerical work, changed because the senior officers could not have a day-to-day detailed knowledge of the progress of the business, so the need to prepare management information brought about the need for returns. Thus the secretarial department was born, and to it was added the calculation of wages and gradually the evolving legislation surrounding this field of activity. Staff records have become of great importance with recent industrial relations legislation and it is nice to think that Crosville, and indeed many bus companies, had established records of this kind 50 years ago.

The commercial side of the business was developing with timetables to publish, publicity to issue, and most important of all, from 1931 onwards, road service licences to organise with the implications of objections, agreements and relationships with other operators and local authorities. So it was that the traffic department evolved and with it the traffic manager who considers his role as that of the person who is responsible for earning the money to keep the company in business. Crosville was, however, organised on the basis of a traffic manager for the Welsh area – Capt E. Roberts – and a similar officer for the English area, H. H. Merchant. The latter became traffic manager of the whole company in 1943 but left in 1945 to take up an appointment as general manager of the Caledonian Omnibus Co of Dumfries. He was succeeded by Capt E. Roberts.

Divisional structure

In addition to the central organisation there were nine divisional managers but this was reduced to seven in 1945 and to five in 1972 despite the acquisition of part of the North Western business. The present arrangements are as follows:-

Divisional Manager Gwynedd, based at Caernarfon
Divisional Manager Clywd, based at Wrexham
Area Traffic Superintendent Mid-Wales, based at Aberystwyth
Divisional Manager Cheshire North West, based at Chester
Divisional Manager Cheshire South East, based at Crewe
Divisional Manager Merseyside, based at Rock Ferry

There is an engineering management structure and with the depot superintendents this enables Crosville to maintain an organisation which has the benefits of central control with local representation at various levels, thereby ensuring a knowledge and responsiveness to local needs.

Welfare and social clubs

Crosville was early in having welfare facilities for staff, and the first sick club was formed at Nantwich in 1922. Benefits of 15s (75p) was payable for 6d (2½p) per week. This was followed by a small mess room – also at Nantwich – and in March 1927 premises were rented above Burton's shop in Foregate Street, Chester, and occupied by a Crosville club, fully-licensed and equipped with billiards tables; due to its location, though, it was unsuccessful and was closed. It was not until 1935 that social clubs were placed on a proper basis, and within two years premises had been provided at Crewe, Wrexham, Oswestry, Llandudno Town, Caernarfon and Llandudno Junction. In 1938 clubs were established at Rhyl and Chester and the first post-war club to be built was at Rock Ferry in 1948. Under the new arrangement the clubs were on company premises, with Crosville paying the rates and financing the building but with the staff running the club. Outside members are permitted to join and today most of the company's depots have a club, the one at Crewe now having fine purpose-built premises constructed during the 1950s.

Through the social clubs came the sporting interest with inter-depot and inter-company football leagues. Other sporting activities are arranged, particularly billiards, snooker and bowls matches.

Although the sick schemes still continue there is a pension and superannuation scheme for staff – Bus Employees Superannuation Trust – organised for all subsidiaries of the National Bus Company. It should be recorded that in 1936 Crosville employees were offered a pension scheme instead of a wage award, but at the time it was decided to accept the improved rate of pay. A salaried staff pension scheme was introduced in 1952.

During the war servicemen in uniform were allowed to use the club and canteen facilities provided for the company's staff; it saved on rations – a great help to households in the wartime situation. On the debit side, it was in the club at Crescent Road

depot, Rhyl, that the disastrous fire started in the early hours of
16 July 1945.

Wages and conditions

Today wages and conditions of platform staff are negotiated at
national level through the auspices of the National Council for
the Omnibus Industry, but this was not always so and rates of
pay, hours worked, etc, varied from one company to another. In
1919 Crosville paid 10s 4d (52p) per weekday, 12s 6d (62½p)
extra if Saturday was worked and 15s 0d (75p) for a Sunday – £4
9s 6d (£4.47½p) for a full week of seven days. There was no
overtime, spreadover, or other payments, but it should be noted
that Saturdays were paid at well over double time and, of course,
were very popular. Bank holidays counted as Saturdays.

Trades union membership

By 1923 the Municipal & General Workers' Union was
organising staff at one or two depots and in due course the
Transport & General Workers' Union became involved. At this
time wages rates for all trades were much lower in Wales than in
England and this situation applied to Crosville, which had as
many as five grades of wages. Anglesey was the worst paid area,
and the reason for this wage variation was the very thin level of
trade which could not support the level of wages paid in
England.

First union agreement

Crosville entered into an agreement with the Transport &
General Workers' Union, but the evolution of industrial
relations was interrupted by the General Strike in 1926,
although not all Crosville depots stopped work. Acquisition of
other operators, the takeover by the LMS, and further expansion
resulted in the company becoming a very large employer. With
the revision and organisation of schedules it became increasingly

apparent that payments must be by the hour, so in 1932 Claude Crosland-Taylor and W. J. Crosland-Taylor met Ernest Bevin and Tom McLean from the Transport & General Workers' Union together with about twelve representatives from the various depots, with the result that the first hourly rate agreement was established.

Railway 'loaned staff'

The merger with Western Transport brought into Crosville employment a number of 'loaned staff' who belonged to the National Union of Railwaymen. These men had railway rates of pay and privileges and were based at Wrexham, Johnstown, Corwen, Oswestry, Pwllheli, Aberystwyth, Machynlleth, and Dolgellau. A better built-in mechanism for dispute could hardly be imagined, and the Crosville board of directors decided to offer cash compensation to those NUR members who would renounce their rights and become members of the Transport & General Workers' Union, working under the terms of the agreement negotiated in 1932. So on 1 August 1933 the big trek took place around the depots, and by the evening all had signed with the exception of Inspector Brooker at Aberystwyth.

National Council for the Omnibus Industry

Crosvilles' first war-time rise in wages was 4s 0d (20p) per week on 20 December 1939 and, at the instigation of the Ministry of Labour and National Service, the employers and trades unions formed the National Council for the Omnibus Industry in 1940 in order to deal with the wages question on a national basis. The first action of the National Council was to conclude a 'Standstill Agreement' under which it was arranged that during the war basic rates would remain the same, and any adjustments of the war wage would be fixed by the NCOI and recommended to their members. On 23 July 1941 the war bonus became 11s 0d (55p) per week. It is interesting to note that this became an annual settlement and may have established the principle of post-war annual wage increments. It was Crosville policy gradually to level-up the wages in the Welsh areas to the English level, and this was accomplished by December 1942.

War bonus

On 7 July 1943 the war bonus increased to £1 0s 0d per week, having reached 15s 0d (75p) per week in March 1942. The Crosville management was already concerned that wage rates were increasing faster than the cost of living.

The tensions of war brought industrial troubles, both towards the end of the war and in the first year of peace. On 7 April 1945 there was trouble at Llandudno, and a stoppage at Bangor soon spread to all Crosville depots as far south as Barmouth. This was followed on 21 January 1947 by a 24-hour stoppage at Crewe. A rumour of short pay stopped work at Mold in February 1947 and at Easter in the same year, Wrexham depot was out for four days.

Post-war reductions in hours, and industrial problems

Wage rates continued to increase on an annual basis, and in 1947 there was a request for a reduction in the 48-hour week to 44 hours at the same rates of pay. On 6 June 1947 the 44-hour week was granted, and as a number of other items were refused strikes occurred at all Crosville's English depots except Liverpool, but at only two Welsh depots, Mold and Flint. This dispute lasted a fortnight, and the next stoppage of any length lasted from 10 to 16 March 1952 at Crewe in a dispute over the employment of conductresses.

It would be tedious to record the individual disputes which have occurred in a form of business which is so varied. Shifts are not 0600 – 1400 and 1400 – 2200 because passenger movement is not like that. It has peaks and troughs, and the public requires transport to suit its needs. Routes and vehicles vary and all sorts of problems arise. These are generally settled without difficulty at local level, and central committees for the various grades of employees deal with matters on a company basis. In general terms industrial relations are good and Crosville, together with other bus companies, have had negotiating machinery in existence for many years, the like of which has only recently been introduced to some other industries as a result of legislation.

Improved conditions

A substantial proportion of Crosville stage carriage mileage is undertaken with one-man-operated buses. This process of conversion has not been an easy process, but within a few years the bus conductor will probably be unknown except in very special circumstances. There is a one-man bonus paid to all platform staff where there is agreement to the operation of these buses, while additional percentages are paid to reflect the type of operation and vehicle used. The basic week came down to 42 hours and is now established at 40 with enhanced payments for various types of work, including payment for unsocial hours. The level of wages has also been effected by the progressive reduction of the permitted number of hours a driver may drive. The trades unions pressed for the remuneration to be maintained even though the number of hours previously worked could not be continued.

Non platform staff conditions

There are now national negotiating arrangements for the salaries, wages and terms of employment of management staff, supervisory, administrative and clerical staff. These agreements have not been brought about without a struggle, helped to some extent by legislation embodied in the Trade Union & Labour Relations Act of 1974.

Ticket-issuing equipment

Besides the standard Setright ticket machines and the fareboxes (now withdrawn) Crosville has carried out experiments with a number of other systems, beginning in 1972 with the experimental use of Videmat machines for comparison with fareboxes on the M22 between Conwy and Old Colwyn. The experiment was not considered a success and the Videmats were soon withdrawn. Although Crosville owns a number of Almex machines, they are only in use on the 'Traws Cambria' service.

As a sequel to the experiment in the fifties with a number of Ultimate machines, it is interesting to note that Crosville is again using Ultimates (owned by the Merseyside PTE) and using its tickets on the H99 rail interchange service in Liverpool. Crosville 'Ultimate tickets' were used for many years on a school service at Runcorn, the tickets being sold at the school and handed to the driver of the bus at time of travel.

Perhaps the most interesting experiment is the Timtronic ticket machine developed by Ticket Equipment Ltd to meet a National Bus Company specification. The machine's most important feature is that it is completely electronic rather than mechanical, and it has a computer memory which dispenses with drivers having to refer to faretables. In addition, transactions are recorded on a module (which replaces the waybill) for subsequent processing in order to obtain the necessary statistical records. Introduced by Crosville some two years ago at Denbigh depot, the use of the machine was extended from 23 May 1980 to all scheduled journeys on the joint Crosville/National Welsh 'Traws Cambria' service and at Ellesmere Port depot. The machine resembles a large electronic calculator and contains a programmed fare module which retains a detailed faretable for the route, or group of routes, including fare concessions. The passenger must state the destination rather than the fare payable, and as the driver presses a key each time he passes a fare stage the machine will automatically compute the fare when the driver punches in the destination stage of the passenger. Where one person is paying for several passengers the machine will compute the total amount payable. Obviously a route such as the 'Traws Cambria', which crosses eight counties, is an ideal application of the machine when the number of concessionary and special fares available is considered.

Gwasanaethau newydd o amgylch Llandudno yn dechrau 16 Tachwedd 1980

New bus services around Llandudno Starting 16th November 1980

L1, M1, M2, M5, M10, M11, M13, M16, M18, M19, M20, M25

CROSVILLE
a **NATIONAL** bus company

Bilingual cover to Welsh service leaflet.

Bi-lingual timetables and bus stops

In 1976 timetables issued in Crosville's Welsh areas were printed with a bi-lingual cover bearing the title 'TAFLEN AMSER TIME TABLE' and bi-lingual service headings. A number of other notices and information displays are displayed in both languages. Originally Crosville used, in common with numerous other operators, a simple white plate with black lettering 'BUS STOP', with the addition of special signs headed

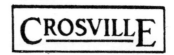

at locations where there was a need to distinguish queuing points to bus stops on allocated services, particularly at bus stations. Timetable frames of various sizes were used and until the early nineteen fifties these showed the actual minutes the buses would depart from that stop. The insets were typed on a special typewriter at the head office at Chester. In the fifties single-sided copies of timetables were glued to backing sheets and the preceding timing point nearest to the stop was underlined, but this practice has now ceased, although timetables extracts are the current method of display except on special locations.

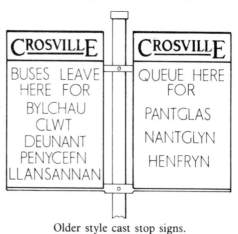

Older style cast stop signs.

The bus stop signs themselves have changed and the national standard pattern is followed, with 'Crosville' and the 'National Bus' logo in white on a green background at the base of the sign. In the Welsh counties bus stop signs of a type approved by the Welsh office are used. They have the words 'Bus Stop' and below (except in Gwynedd, where the county insists the Welsh name is above the English) the Welsh equivalent 'Safle Bysiau'.

Welsh Office approved sign as used in Welsh counties except Gwynedd where Welsh precedes the English.

In the sixties there was an intermediate stage with a vertical sign in three versions:-

White background with 'BUS STOP' in black
Yellow background with 'BUS STOP IN AND OUT' in black
This was used to denote stops on either side of the road with one post and sign.
Blue background with 'ALL BUS AND LIMITED STOP SERVICES' also in black

There is also a double-sided rectangular sign with green lettering 'CROSVILLE EXPRESS SERVICE STOP' on an orange background.

From left to right: Standard stop sign (single sided); Dual purpose sign (single sided); Limited stop sign (single sided); sign used to mark Crosville stops in Merseyside Passenger Transport Executive area (attached to PTE poles).

Advertising on buses

As previously mentioned, this came about with Tilling control in 1942 and has been extended to cover 'overall' advertising buses. Revenue from this source makes a worthwhile contribution to the company's income. An interesting series of announcements was arranged during the war for publication in the local press in order to try and make the public understand why buses were overcrowded and travelling uncomfortable. By reason of a contact made by Mr W. J. Crosland-Taylor with Mr Douglas England, who illustrated the 'charivaria' page of *Punch*, it was arranged that Mr Crosland-Taylor would write the words which Mr Douglas England would illustrate. Nearly one hundred were published and formed a very valuable part of Crosville's public relations efforts during the dark days of the war. As early as the nineteen fifties a number of buses carried lower rear advertisements printed in Welsh. One was for Vernons football pools with the slogan – 'POSTIWICH I VERNONS'. (Post it to Vernons).

CROSVILLE EXPRESS SERVICE STOP

Express coach stop sign, (double sided).

Cafes and catering

Crosville has always been active in this respect, commencing with the bus stations at Heswall. Over the years the catering department has maintained cafeterias and other facilities at a number of locations throughout the company's operating area, but these are now run by outside caterers.

Traffic trainees

In the early thirties Crosville commenced a scheme to train young men for future management positions. Each trainee was required to undergo five years' training in the various departments, and in addition to being required to successfully pass both the general managers' and the Chartered Institute of Transport examinations, was also expected to qualify as both a bus driver and conductor. Many of the former trainees hold senior posts in the National Bus Co, which has a wide ranging series of training schemes for staff at all levels.

Crosville United

In the years after the war the company established an internal staff magazine called *Crosville United*. It appeared four times each year and contained an opening message from the general manager, with articles on the company's buses – past and present, and other matters regarding the company of interest to the staff. It featured a large section for individual department and depot news. When the National Bus Company's *Bus* newspaper was introduced *Crosville United*, along with magazines produced by a number of other NBC subsidiary companies, ceased publication in its original form, but single-sheet editions are issued from time to time.

Travel agencies and enquiry offices

Beside the usual enquiry offices dealing in the main with the company's business and bookings on other facilities provided by the National Bus Company, Crosville maintains ABTA 'travel agencies' at head office, Chester, Heswall, Crewe bus station, Chester bus station, Runcorn (Shopping City) and Wrexham (King Street). An interesting feature of enquiry offices is the sending of 'parcels by bus'. This is a great convenience to many small communities and businesses. Before the legalising of betting shops, bets collected by bookies' runners were placed in special locked boxes – about the size of a shoe box – and thinly disguised as parcels, were sent to their destinations by Crosville bus. The conveyance of newspapers by bus is an important feature in the areas covered.

Data processing

Until 1971 Crosville utilised NCR and Logabax equipment in its Chester Head Office to support a broad range of clerical systems. In that year it was agreed that the computer facilities available to Ribble Motor Services should be shared between the two companies. These facilities were provided by a separate NBC subsidiary, Scout Computer Services, which was based in Preston, having evolved from Ribble's own internal computer department. In 1977 Scout Computer Services was incorporated into the new subsidiary NBC Computer Services Limited.

The current situation has remained basically unchanged since 1974. The company rents an MDS key-to-disc installation housed in its head office, which is linked to the mainframe computer (an ICL 1902T) at Preston by private telephone line. The MDS equipment is used for data preparation of the Company's computerised systems. Once keyed, the data is stored until ready for transmission. It is then transmitted to Preston, processed on the mainframe computer, and the results transmitted back to Chester for the reports to be printed on-site. All the computer systems are therefore batch systems, and the clerical procedures have been adapted to reflect the turn-round time required to process them.

The first computer systems introduced into the Company were Ribble systems adapted to suit the requirements of Crosville. These systems covered payroll, stock control, waybill processing and creditors' ledger. During the past six years these original systems have been modified either to improve their efficiency or to cater for the Company's changing requirements. In addition, new systems have been developed for operational costing, scholars' and period tickets, cash book, debtors' ledger and vehicle maintenance costing (VMC).

At the time of writing the company employed some 1,800 drivers, 350 conductors, 700 engineering staff (fitters, body builders, painters and cleaners etc) and just over 500 supervisory and clerical staff (including inspectors, clerks, superintendants and mangers) to operate a fleet of 1,100 buses on some 830 stage carriage services. 306 services are of an urban nature, 68 are inter-urban and 456 are rural. Within an operating area of 7,000 square miles the company's vehicles worked some 36,994,000 miles in 1979 and 87,786,000 passenger journeys were made. Traffic revenue in that financial year amounted to £26,579,000 and support payments totalled £4,072,000. Whilst these statistics are very impressive they make sombre reading when it is considered that in 1947, with a similar number of vehicles, the company operated an almost identical mileage (36,726,787) but 158,490,453 passenger journeys were made.

Appendices

Businesses (whole or in part) added to the original Crosville Motor Co. Ltd. and subsequently to Crosville Motor Services Ltd.

Name	Place	Date	Main Routes Only
Lightfoot	Kelsall	—.—.11	Kelsall–Chester
Gregory	Crewe	—. 1.15	Nantwich–Crewe–Sandbach
Ward Bros	Crewe	—.—.15	Crewe Town
J. M. Hudson	Ellesmere Port	27. 1.22	Ellesmere Port–Chester
J. Pye	Heswall	1. 1.24	Birkenhead–Heswall Birkenhead–Parkgate
D. M. Jenkins	Aberaeron	21. 2.25	Aberaeron–New Quay
J. Gibson	Crewe	6. 4.25	Crewe–Audley Nantwich–Crewe–Sandbach
Gauterin Bros	Farndon	26.10.25	Farndon–Chester
Richards (Busy Bee)	Caernarfon	9.11.25	Caernarfon–Pwllheli
A. Harding	Birkenhead	—.11.25	Birkenhead–Heswall
Hooker	Aberaeron	—.11.25	Aberaeron–Cardigan
Abraham Lloyd	Queensferry	11. 3.26	Queensferry–Chester
Trevor Garner	Runcorn	10. 2.27	Runcorn local
Joseph Rogers	Malpas	10. 2.27	Malpas–Chester
Hugh Jones	Penmachno	10. 2.27	Llanrwst–Penmachno
A. & R. Motors	Criccieth	1.10.27	Porthmadog–Pwllheli
J. Lewis Owens	Caernarfon	10.11.27	Nevin–Edeyrn
A. V. Peach	Haslington	10.11.27	Haslington–Crewe
Don Taylor	Haslington	10.11.27	Haslington–Crewe
Peris Motors	Caernarfon	—.10.28	Caernarfon–Llanberis
Thos. John Edwards	Caernarfon	—.10.28	Caernarfon–Bryn Refail
Cynfi Motors	Deiniolen	11. 7.29	Caernarfon–Dinorwic

Name	Place	Date	Main Routes Only
Holyhead Motors (Mona Maroon)	Holyhead	4.11.29	Holyhead–Valley Holyhead–South Stack Holyhead–Rhoscolyn Holyhead–Cemaes–Amlwch (four routes) Holyhead–Llangefni–Benllech
UNU	Llangefni	1. 1.30	Caernarfon–Beaumaris Bangor–Holyhead Bangor–Newborough Bangor–Llangefni Caernarfon–Birkenhead Caernarfon–Bangor Caernarfon–Menai Bridge Newborough
Brookes Bros	Rhyl	1. 5.30	All round Rhyl
W. Edwards	Denbigh	31. 7.30	Ruthin–Clocaenog Ruthin–Hiraethog Caerwys–Station Denbigh–Llanrhaiadr Denbigh–Tremeirchion Abergele–Rhyl Denbigh–Ruthin–Corwen Denbigh–Bylchau Denbigh–Prion Saron
C. Burton	Tarporley	31. 7.30	Chester–Tarporley
N. Wales Silver	Llandudno	1. 8.30	Llandudno–Colwyn Bay–Abergele Llandudno–Conwy Landudno–Alexandra Road Llandudno–Betws-y-Coed Colwyn Bay–Llysfaen Colwyn Bay–Betws-yn-Rhos
Llangoed Red	Beaumaris	1.10.30	Bangor–Llangoed–Penmon
Vincent Smith	Prestatyn	29. 1.31	Hillside–Beach
H. C. Pascoe	Tarporley	31. 1.31	Tarporley–Northwich
Zacchaeus Woodfin	Tarvin	2. 2.31	Chester–Tarporley via Christleton Chester–Burton via Huxley Barrow–Chester
Ribble Motors (Liverpool–London)	Preston	5. 2.31	Liverpool–London
Llandudno Coaching	Llandudno	18. 2.31	Llandudno and Bangor Blue

178

Name	Place	Date	Main Routes Only
Bethesda Greys	Bethesda	1. 1.32	Rachub–Bethesda
			Bangor–Gerlan
			(five routes)
			Bangor–Bethesda
			Douglas Hill–Bethesda
			Douglas Hill–Bangor
J. W. Hughes	Rhiwen	15. 1.32	Caernarfon–Rhiwlas
			Bangor–Llanberis
			Caernarfon–Dinorwic
Caernarvon Bay Motors	Caernarfon	6.12.32	Caernarfon–Dinas Dinlle
Roses Tours	Rhyl	—. 2.33	Tours from Rhyl
Western Transport	Wrexham	1. 5.33	All Wrexham, etc
Jones Bros	Aberystwyth	1. 5.33	Aberystwyth–Aberaeron
			Aberystwyth–Lampeter
			Aberystwyth–Borth
			Aberystwyth–Tregaron
			Aberystwyth–Ponterwyd
Wm. Lloyd	Beddgelert	14. 6.33	Beddgelert–Porthmadog
Seiont Motors	Caernarfon	1. 1.34	Caernarfon–Penygroes–Nantlle
Jas Rothwell	Holt	1. 1.34	Wrexham–Holt
			Wrexham–Broxton
Red & White	London	8. 1.34	London–Liverpool
Wirral Motor Transport	Birkenhead	10. 2.34	Birkenhead–Bangor
Nevin Blue	Nevin	15. 2.34	Pwllheli–Nevin–Edeyrn
D. J. Williams (Mynytho)	Pwllheli	15. 2.34	Mynytho–Llanbedrog Pwllheli
Tocia Motor Co. Ltd	Aberdaron	17. 2.34	Pwllheli–Criccieth–Abersoch
			Aberdaron–Llanbedrog–Llangian
Wm. Morris	Bethesda	23. 5.34	Bangor–Rhiwlas
R. T. Jones	Llanrwst	1. 6.34	Llanrwst–Trefriw–Capel Garmon–Melin-y-coed
S. Jackson & Sons	Crewe	26. 6.34	Nantwich–Wettenhall–Winsford
			Nantwich–Crewe–Sandbach
			Crewe–Valley Road
T. O. Maddocks	Tattenhall	1. 7.34	Bunbury–Chester
			Broxton–Chester
			Tattenhall–Chester
			Tattenhall–Whitchurch
W. J. Jones	Rhiw	2. 7.34	Pwllheli–Rhiw

Appendices

Name	Place	Date	Main Routes Only
J. D. Davies	Llangybi	20. 7.34	Aberystwyth–Tregaron–Lampeter
H. Lowe & Son	Audlem	1. 8.34	Audlem–Drayton Audlem–Nantwich Audlem–Whitchurch
R. Jenkinson	Buckley	19. 9.34	Buckley–Chester Infirmary Buckley–Mold Buckley–Connah's Quay Mold–Alltami
Macdonald & Co	Birkenhead	1.12.34	Birkenhead–Caernarfon etc
J. W. Garner	Runcorn	1. 1.35	Runcorn local and Helsby
F. Watson	Runcorn	1. 1.35	Runcorn local
R. Roberts	Pwllheli	11. 2.35	Pwllheli–Uwchmynydd Pwllheli–Garn Chapel
H. O. Owens	Pwllheli	11. 2.35	Pwllheli–Dinas
Tudor Evans	Llithfaen	25. 2.35	Edeyrn–Nevin–Llithfaen–Caernarfon Llithfaen–Pwllheli
J. A. Richards	Towyn	11. 3.35	Towyn–Bryn Crug–Caerbellan
A. W. Reeves	Oswestry	18. 3.35	Oswestry–Leighton Oswestry–Bagley Oswestry–Treflach
D. H. Tyler	Oswestry	18. 3.35	Oswestry–Nant Mawr Oswestry–Sychtyn
J. B. S. Platt	Oswestry	18. 3.35	Oswestry–Trefonen and Bryn
W. B. Jones	Oswestry	18. 3.35	Oswestry–New Martin Oswestry–Sodylt Bank Oswestry–Duddleston Heath Ellesmere–Duddleston Ellesmere–Ifton
New Blue	Llandudno Junction	11. 4.35	Conwy–Llandudno Conwy–Colwyn Bay Fforddlas Bridge–Colwyn Bay
J. Price	Wrexham	15. 4.35	Rhos–Blackpool Rhos–Rhyl Wrexham–Llay Main–Caergwrle Wrexham–Tanyfron Wrexham–Cymmau
H. Williams	Shop Uchaf	1. 5.35	Rhydwen–Holyhead
H. Williams	Glyn Afon	1. 5.35	Glyn Afon–Holyhead

Name	Place	Date	Main Routes Only
Evan Owen	Garreglefn	1. 5.35	Amlwch–Llangefni
J. H. Roberts	Trevor	1. 5.35	Llangefni–Holyhead
J. Roberts	Gwalchmai	1. 5.35	Llangefni–Holyhead
G. R. Parry	Llanddeusant	1. 5.35	Amlwch–Holyhead
Pearson, Jones & Horn	Liverpool	25. 5.35	Southport–Liverpool–London
Mechell Maroon	Anglesey	5. 6.35	Bangor–Cemaes Holyhead–Cemaes etc
Albert Mates	Chirk	30.11.35	Chirk–Cefn Mawr
Iorwerth Evans	Llanrhaiadr	21.12.35	Oswestry–Llanrhaiadr
John Hughes	Carmel	25. 1.36	Caernarfon–Cilgwyn
G. Roberts	Southsea	28. 1.36	Wrexham–Bradley Wrexham–Rhyl
G. A. Williams	Cefn	3. 2.36	Cefn–Chirk Cefn–Ellesmere
D. M. Prichard	Llanrug	1. 3.36	Caernarfon–Llanberis Caernarfon–Bethesda
W. D. Humphreys	Bethel	1. 3.36	Caernarfon–Bethel
S. Williams & Sons	Pentre Broughton	15. 6.36	Wrexham–Pentre Broughton
E. J. Hughes	Pen-y-groes	15. 6.36	Pen-y-groes–Dinas Dinlle
David Jones	Newborough	15. 6.36	Llangefni–Newborough
Jones' Motor Services	Flint	15. 6.36	Bagillt–Flint–Shotton
Harold Roberts	Connah's Quay	6. 7.36	Flint–Sandycroft
Crowther & Co	Shotton	12. 1.37	Flint–Sandycroft
Davies Bros	Tanygrisiau	15. 3.37	Ffestiniog–Tanygrisiau
C. H. Williams	Rock Ferry	22. 7.37	Tours from Birkenhead
J. R. Lloyd	Bwlchgwyn	2. 5.38	Wrexham–Bwlchgwyn Wrexham–Gwynfryn
Alfred Wright	Rhosymedre	1. 3.39	Chirk–Cefn Mawr Chirk–Glyn Valley
H. Stanley	Buckley	1. 3.39	Buckley–Shotton Mold–Llay Main
L. J. Roberts	Llanrug	30. 6.39	Caernarfon–Ceunant
C. W. Shone	Bangor Isycoed	1. 3.40	Wrexham–Isycoed
D. S. Rogers	Coedpoeth	15. 5.40	Wrexham–Coedpoeth
H. Hooson	Coedpoeth	15. 5.40	Wrexham–Coedpoeth
I. T. Roberts	Coedpoeth	15. 5.40	Wrexham–Coedpoeth
Owen Roberts	Colwyn Bay	1. 2.41	Colwyn Bay–Brynymaen
O. Glyn Parry	Benllech	11. 8.41	Llangefni–Benllech
Primrose Motors	Aberystwyth	—. 4.46	Aberystwyth–Cwm Erfin
F. W. Strange	Wrexham	9. 3.47	Wrexham–Pandy
Mrs. E. Williams	Marchwiel	1. 1.51	Wrexham–Overton Wrexham–Tallarn Green Wrexham–Pilgrims Place Ellesmere–Northwood

Name	Place	Date	Main Routes Only
Mrs. M. Ellis	Llanllechid	3. 2.52	Gerlan end Rachub–Bangor
Davies Bros	Summerhill	20. 2.53	Wrexham–Buckley Wrexham–Summerhill
G. Sugg	Garden Village Wrexham	26. 4.54	Wrexham–Garden Village
W. T. & E. Keeler	Garden Village Wrexham	26. 4.54	Wrexham–Garden Village
Llandudno & Colwyn Bay Electric Rly Co Ltd	Rhos-on-Sea	28. 5.61	Llandudno–Colwyn Bay
J. W. Lloyd & Sons Ltd	Oswestry	16.10.61	Oswestry–Black Park Woodside–Middleton Road School
R. Johnson & Sons	Wrexham	22.10.61	Wrexham–Southsea–Coedpoeth Excursions & tours from Southsea
Meredith & Jesson Ltd	Cefn Mawr	8. 4.69	Cefn–Wrexham
Mid-Wales Motorways Ltd			Excursions & tours from Cefn Mawr
North Western	Biddulph, Macclesfield & Northwich	1. 1.72	North Cheshire and South Lancashire
Mid-Wales Motorways Ltd	Shrewsbury	15. 2.72	Four Crosses–Shrewsbury Shrewsbury–Newtown
Western Welsh	Newcastle Emlyn New Quay	23. 4.72	Services in South Cardinganshire
South Wales Transport	Lampeter	23. 4.72	Aberystwyth–Ammanford
Lancashire United Transport	none	27. 4.74	Warrington area
J. Phillips & Son Rhostyllen	Rhostyllen	—.—.79	Wrexham–Tainant Wrexham–Rhos

APPENDIX II

Location of depots and sub-depots giving the year in which the premises were occupied and the allocation of buses in 1947 and 1980.

	Date Opened	Open Feb. 1980	Allocation of Vehicles March 1947	Allocation of Vehicles Feb. 1980
Aberaeron	1929	Yes	4	11
Aberdaron	1934	No	2	NIL
Aberystwyth	1934	Yes	28	21
Amlwch	1935	Yes	11	7
Bangor	1931	Yes	54	42
Barmouth	1924	No	4	NIL
Biddulph	1972	Yes	NIL	13
Birkenhead	1932	Yes	68	48
Bl. Ffestiniog	1926	Yes	11	5
Bryn Crug	1935	No	3	NIL
Caernarfon	1932	Yes	44	25
Cardigan	1941	No	2	NIL
Chester	1927	Yes	28	65
Congleton	1980	No	NIL	A
Corwen	1934	Yes	8	11
Crewe	1926	Yes	54	60
Criccieth	1927	No	5	NIL
Denbigh	1930	Yes	21	14
Dolgellau	1934	Yes	5	13
Ellesmere Port	1962	Yes	NIL	16
Flint	1937	Yes	47	33
Heswall	1924	Yes	27	39
Holyhead	1930	Yes	9	10
Johnstown	1933	No	19	NIL
Lampeter	1972	Yes	NIL	B
Llandrindod Wells	1928	No	4	NIL
Llandudno Junction	1931	Yes	47	51
Llandudno	1931	No	21	NIL
Llangefni	1930	Yes	7	7
Llanfaircaereinion	1933	No	2	NIL
Llanrhaiadr	1936	No	1	NIL
Llangynog	1933	No	1	NIL
Llangybi	1934	No	1	NIL
Llanidloes	1925	No	2	NIL
Llanrwst	1931	No	13	NIL
Llanrug	1936	No	4	NIL
Liverpool	1928	Yes	67	107
New Quay	1972	No	NIL	NIL
Macclesfield	1972	Yes	NIL	55
Machynlleth	1934	Yes	8	7

Middlewich	1934	No	4	NIL
Mold	1923	Yes	42	33
Nantwich	1915	No	17	NIL
Nevin	1933	No	4	NIL
Newcastle Emlyn	1972	Yes	NIL	6
Newcastle-under-Lyme	1932	Yes	5	C
Northwich	1972	Yes	NIL	50
Oswestry	1933	Yes	14	24
Porthmadog	1936	Yes	6	D
Pwllheli	1934	Yes	15	21
Rhyl	1930	Yes	55	51
Runcorn	1942	Yes	37	61
Warrington	1924	Yes	23	41
West Kirby	1923	Yes	27	40
Wrexham	1933	Yes	103	94

Notes:–

A – Opened when Biddulph closed.

B – Sub-depot of Aberystwyth

C – Sub-depot of Crewe

D – Sub-depot of Caernarfon

E – Different premises have been occupied in the same town from time to time, for instance Crewe depot was at Queen Street until the new bus station was opened.

F – Outstations are not included, many different places have been used over the years in accordance with traffic requirements.

APPENDIX III
Depot allocation discs

About 1932 Crosville introduced a system whereby the division to which a bus was allocated could be readily identified by reference to a small coloured disc mounted on a special raised plate on the rear off-side of the bus. On single-deckers the plate was positioned at roof height and on double-deckers at the level of the cantrail. Originally the scheme provided for the initial letter of the depot to which the bus was allocated to be shown on the disc and the fitting provided for the display of two discs, that for the home depot being on the left-hand side. It was possible to identify for instance a Rock Ferry bus on loan to Barmouth. The depot initials were discontinued at the time of the divisional re-organisation in June 1945. The practice ceased altogether during the early nineteen fifties but the colour coding was as follows:–

Division	Colour	Depots
Chester (1)	White	Chester (Mold and Flint became white in the divisional reorganisation)
Merseyside	Mauve	Liverpool, Rock Ferry, Heswall, West Kirby, Warrington and Runcorn
Crewe	Red	Crewe, Nantwich, Middlewich and Newcastle-under-Lyme
Wrexham	Black	Oswestry, Johnstown and Corwen
Rhyl (2)	Orange	Rhyl, Denbigh, Mold and Flint
Llandudno	Blue	Llandudno Town, Llandudno Junction and Llanwrst
North Cambrian (3)	Yellow	Bangor, Holyhead, Llangefni, Amlwch, Caernarfon, Criccieth and Pwllheli Blaenau Ffestiniog
South Cambrian (3)	Green	Aberystwyth, Aberayron, Machynlleth Llandrindod Wells, Llanidloes, Barmouth and Dolgellau

Notes
(1) With the divisional re-organisation Mold and Flint depots were transferred to Chester division and the buses allocated to these depots received white discs.
(2) When Rhyl and Llandudno divisions were combined a blue disc was substituted for the orange one carried by the buses allocated to the Rhyl and Denbigh depots.
(3) In the original divisional organisation there was a Bangor and South Cambrian division consisting of Bangor, Holyhead, Llangefni, Amlwch and the South Cambrian depots (excluding Barmouth and Dolgellau, which were part of the Caernarfon division until 1945) with a green colour coding. Therefore, with the re-organisation of the divisions, Bangor, Holyhead, Amlwch and Llangefni depots became yellow instead of green, and Barmouth and Dolgellau changed from yellow to green.

185

APPENDIX IV
Summary of various matters referring to vehicles

(A) Leyland LT5A bodies
G1/17 – Tooth 34 seats
G2/3 – Leyland "all-metal" 43 seats
G4–G16 and G18–G21 – ECOC Ltd 32 seats

(B) K6Bs and L6Bs delivered as MB or KB and reclassified MW or KW (later deliveries were MW or KW from new):–
MBs274, 278, 279, 281, 282, 285–294, 310, 318, 320–322
KBs70, 71, 92–95

(C) KAs which had their sides rebuilt by Crosville in 1950 were:–
KAs16, 18–22, 25–28, 37, 41, 46, 57, 60, 63, 66, 70, 71, 74, 75, 77, 81, 83–86
KA47 was rebuilt with full width canopy and jacknife door for one-man operation

(D) Strachans utility bodies were exchanged as follows:–

Body from	to
MB 172	MB 167 (ex LTE)
174	163
175	165
176	168
179	162
187	161

(E) KAs exchanged with Wilts & Dorset in 1952 were:–
KAs 38, 40, 48, 54, 55, 59, 61, 64, 68, 87

(F) Platform doors were fitted to the following Lodekkas
675–81, 722–41, 749–65, 769–810, 812–999 and 1–263

(G) Classification of Bristol MW chassis
SMG 371–85, 391–406, 437–66, 497–509, 533–55 and 587–92
CMG 341, 357–70, 386–90, 407–14, 427–36, 467–92, 510–23, 556–70 and 30–36
EMG 342–56, 415–26 and 581–86

Bibliography

Buses Illustrated/Buses magazine, published by Ian Allan – articles from various editions

Rolling Road by L. A. G. Strong, published by Hutchinson & Co (Publishers) Ltd

The Sowing and the Harvest by W. J. Crosland Taylor, published by Littlebury Bros Ltd

State Owned without Tears by W. J. Crosland Taylor, published by Littlebury Bros Ltd

Commercial Motor, published by IPC Transport Press Ltd – article regarding bus services in Welsh parks

A History of Western National by R. C. Anderson and G. G. A. Frankis, published by David & Charles

A History of the Llandudno and Colwyn Bay Electric Railway Co Ltd by R. C. Anderson, published by the Quail Map Co

Railway Motor Buses and Bus Services in the British Isles 1902–33, Vols 1 and 2 by John Cummings, published by the Oxford Publishing Co

Publicity releases, fleet lists and handbooks published by Crosville Motor Services Ltd

Great British Tramway Networks by W. H. Bett and J. C. Gilham, published by the Light Railway Transport League

1972 Annual Report and Accounts of the South East Lancashire & North East Cheshire Transport Authority and Executive

1968 Annual Report of the Transport Holding Co

1969 to date Annual Reports of the National Bus Co Ltd

Motor Transport (weekly newspaper) published by IPC Transport Press Ltd

Fleet History PC8, Crosville Motor Services Ltd, part II 1935–52, published jointly by the PSV Circle and the Omnibus Society

Bus newspaper, published by the National Bus Co Ltd

Motor Coach Services from Merseyside 1920 to 1940, Parts 1 and 2 by T. B. Maund, published by the Omnibus Society

Freighters on the Front, written and published by David Kaye

187

Index

Index

Index

192